Revealed Preferences

Understanding the Choices That Shape Our Lives

by
Faye Chandler

Faye Chandler

Copyright 2024 Faye Chandler. All Rights reserved. No part of this publication may be reproduced without consent of the author.

"Economists tend to rely on 'revealed preference' rather than verbal statements. That is, what people do reveals what their values are, better than what they say."

-Thomas Sowell

Faye Chandler

Table of Contents

Chapter 1: The Choice Architecture Around Us

Chapter 2: Understanding Revealed Preferences

Chapter 3: The Psychology of Choice

Chapter 4: Cultural Influences and Social Norms

Chapter 5: The Power of Defaults

Chapter 6: Identifying and Recalibrating Your Preferences

Chapter 7: The Digital Influence: Choices in a Tech-Driven World

Chapter 8: The Role of Habits in Decision-Making

Chapter 9: Harnessing the Power of Reflection

Chapter 10: Empowerment Through Informed Choices

Introduction

Have you ever found yourself standing in front of your closet, overwhelmed by choices, yet feeling like you have nothing to wear? Or perhaps you've agonized over a menu, only to order the same dish you always do. These everyday dilemmas reveal a fascinating truth about human nature: our choices are often influenced by forces we can't see or fully understand.

Welcome to "Revealed Preferences," a journey into the hidden world of decision-making. This book is your guide to uncovering the invisible threads that shape our choices, from the clothes we wear to the careers we pursue. By exploring the field of behavioral economics, we'll shine a light on the unconscious influences that drive our preferences and ultimately shape our lives.

Throughout these pages, we'll examine how social norms subtly nudge our decisions, how cognitive biases color our judgment, and how emotions sway our preferences in ways we might not expect. You'll discover why you might choose a familiar brand over a better alternative, or why you sometimes act against your own best interests.

But this book is more than just a fascinating exploration of human behavior. It's a toolkit for transformation. By understanding the mechanisms behind our choices, we gain the power to make decisions that truly align with our values and aspirations. This knowledge is the key to living a more authentic and fulfilling life.

As we progress through each chapter, you'll gain practical insights that you can apply to your daily life. From navigating complex financial decisions to improving your relationships, the principles you'll learn here have the potential to reshape your approach to life's big and small choices alike.

So, are you ready to pull back the curtain on your own decision-making process? To challenge your assumptions and discover new paths to personal growth? Then let's begin this journey together. Welcome to the revealing world of "Revealed Preferences."

Faye Chandler

Chapter 1: The Choice Architecture Around Us

Frameworks of Decision-Making: Store Layouts and Website Designs

Imagine walking into a store where soft music plays in the background, the inviting smell of freshly baked bread fills the air, and warm lighting highlights the latest seasonal items. Almost immediately, whether you planned to or not, you find yourself in a carefully crafted atmosphere meant to sway your choices. This blend of sights, sounds, and scents isn't random; it's the result of thoughtful design, a concept known as "choice architecture."

At the heart of choice architecture is how options are presented to us and how that presentation impacts our decisions. Marketers and designers are well aware of the psychological tricks at work. They create spaces—whether it's a physical store or a digital site—that guide us toward specific choices. While strolling through the aisles of a supermarket or browsing an online shop, you might not even realize how your decisions are gently nudged by the frameworks around you.

One intriguing principle in this area is the decoy effect. Picture yourself in a café, faced with a small coffee for $2.50, a medium for $3.00, and a large for $4.00. Now, imagine the café adds a fourth option: a gigantic "super-size" coffee for $5.00, loaded with caffeine. This less appealing option—the super-size coffee—changes how you view the other choices. Suddenly, the medium coffee, which once seemed only a bit pricier than the small, starts to look like a much better deal. This clever strategy prompts many people to choose the medium size, even if they initially intended to grab the small.

Retailers have long taken advantage of this psychological quirk. In one memorable example, a popular electronics store showcased three TV models. The first was a basic 32-inch model priced at $500, the second—a 50-inch version—cost $1,000. The third option, a lavish 65-inch model, was set at a tempting $2,000. The presence of the extravagant 65-inch TV changed how people made decisions. Faced with the high price of the top-tier model, many shoppers found themselves leaning toward the 50-inch option, believing it was the most sensible choice. Retailers know that by cleverly placing a decoy, they can steer customers' choices, making them think they are making smart decisions when, really, they are guided by these well-planned nudges.

Another important principle is anchoring, which affects how choice architecture is designed. The anchoring effect happens when the first piece of information you see influences your future judgments and decisions. For instance, if you walk into a jewelry store and first see a gorgeous diamond ring priced at $10,000, that figure influences how you view other rings priced at $5,000 or even $3,000. Suddenly, what might have seemed like a huge purchase feels more justifiable.

In the world of online shopping, anchoring can look a bit different. Many e-commerce sites display a "regular price" crossed out next to a "sale price." Our eyes are naturally drawn to the higher number, which acts as an anchor and makes the sale price seem like a fantastic deal. The psychological effect is significant; shoppers might think they're saving money, even if the sale price is still above what they originally planned to spend. This way, the anchoring effect can skew our perception and lead to impulse buys that don't align with what we actually wanted.

Sensory experiences in retail environments also play a big role in choice architecture. Imagine stepping into a high-end department store; everything is designed to make you feel luxurious and desired. Soft lighting creates a welcoming vibe, while carefully chosen scents evoke feelings of comfort or aspiration. For example, many upscale brands use scented candles or diffusers to engage your sense of smell, creating an exclusive and appealing atmosphere.

Consider a luxury cosmetics store. From the moment you walk in, you're surrounded by delightful fragrances, calming music, and an elegant layout that showcases products in an almost magical way. The soothing background music slows shoppers down, making them more inclined to indulge in high-end purchases. The setting encourages customers to linger, explore, and ultimately, buy.

On the flip side, picture a no-frills discount retailer where the layout is kept simple. Here, the focus shifts from creating a captivating experience to ensuring efficiency. Bright lights, minimal sounds, and products displayed for quick access are the norm. The goal isn't to enchant; it's to provide a fast and practical shopping experience. Each of these sensory experiences, whether lavish or straightforward, affects how we make our choices once we step inside the store.

Shifting from physical stores to online spaces, choice architecture remains just as significant, if not more. Website design plays a vital role in shaping user experiences. A well-organized website can either simplify the decision-making process or make it more complicated.

A website focused on user experience usually boasts a clean design, easy navigation, and visual cues that lead users toward desired actions. For example, an online store might highlight a limited-time offer with a countdown timer, creating a sense of urgency. This simple design element can prompt users to make quicker decisions. The looming deadline nudges them toward impulse purchases, tapping into the psychological principle of loss aversion—the fear of missing out often overshadows rational thinking about whether the purchase is truly needed.

Take a popular online clothing retailer, for instance. When you arrive on their homepage, you're greeted with a featured product and a clear button that says "Shop Now." As you scroll, you see carefully organized sections showcasing customer favorites, seasonal must-haves, and special deals. This thoughtful layout captures your interest without overwhelming you. The streamlined design not only makes navigation easy but also effectively encourages users to decide to buy.

In contrast, a cluttered website filled with ads, pop-ups, and too much information can confuse users. Feeling overwhelmed by choices and distractions, they might abandon their shopping cart entirely. This makes clear the importance of well-considered website design that prioritizes the user's experience.

Understanding the frameworks of choice architecture, whether in physical stores or online, helps us become aware of how our decisions are often shaped by outside influences. By recognizing the psychological principles at play, we can become more mindful of how we make choices. The aim isn't to eliminate choice but to empower ourselves to navigate the complexities of our decisions with greater awareness and clarity.

Next time you find yourself picking out products, whether in a beautifully lit store or on a well-designed website, take a moment to consider how you might be subtly influenced by the choices presented to you. With this knowledge, you can approach your decisions more thoughtfully, ensuring that they truly reflect your values and desires, rather than simply responding to the clever tactics of choice architects. You can acknowledge and understand the invisible hand guiding your choices, ultimately steering you toward a more genuine experience.

The Subtle Art of Nudging: Behavioral Prompts in Action

In the world of human decision-making, nudging is a clever tool that works quietly in the background, guiding our choices without taking away our freedom. Think of it as a gentle push instead of a strong shove. A subtle nudge can help us make decisions that are better for us, often without us even noticing it. This idea has gained popularity in recent years, thanks in large part to researchers Richard Thaler and Cass Sunstein. Their book, "Nudge: Improving Decisions About Health, Wealth, and Happiness," helps us understand how nudges operate and how they can impact our lives significantly.

So, what is a nudge, exactly? A nudge can be any small change in how choices are presented that leads to a change in behavior, all without taking away options or significantly changing economic incentives. For example, think about a cafeteria that puts fruits at eye level while placing desserts on lower shelves. This simple setup nudges us toward healthier eating choices. The way options are arranged can have a big effect on what we pick, often guiding us toward decisions that boost our well-being.

The charm of nudging lies in its straightforwardness and grace. It honors our ability to choose while gently steering us toward smarter decisions. Unlike traditional persuasion methods that might rely on fear or pressure, nudging takes a kinder approach. It understands that humans don't always act rationally; our choices can be swayed by our emotions, biases, and our surroundings. Nudges can remind us of our intentions, helping us align our actions with what we truly value.

Nudging can be applied in many areas, showcasing its flexibility and effectiveness. One compelling example is in healthcare. Take the organ donation program. In countries like Spain, the default is set to be an organ donor unless someone chooses to opt out. As a result, participation rates are much higher compared to countries like the United States, where people must actively choose to be donors. This seemingly small change in presenting choices leads to life-saving results. By simply changing the default setting, policymakers can encourage people to make decisions that reflect a sense of community and altruism.

The financial sector has also seen remarkable results from nudging. A great example of this is automatic enrollment in retirement savings plans. Research shows that when employees are enrolled automatically in these plans, participation rates dramatically increase compared to voluntary enrollment. The nudge is clear: by making enrollment automatic, people are more likely to save for retirement, which helps them avoid the procrastination that often comes with making active choices. This isn't just about saving money; it's also about securing a stable financial future and nudging individuals toward a more prosperous life.

Real-world nudging goes beyond just healthcare and finance; it seeps into our everyday lives. Think about your last trip to the grocery store. If the store is designed with nudging principles, healthier options like fresh fruits and vegetables might be placed near the entrance, while sugary snacks are hidden on higher shelves. This encourages shoppers to make healthier choices right from the start. Similarly, restaurants often design their menus to nudge customers. By placing the most profitable dishes at the top or highlighting certain items, they guide customers toward choices that benefit both their health and the restaurant's success.

Nudging can also be seen in our digital lives. Online shopping platforms often use nudges to improve user experiences and boost sales. A classic example is a "limited-time offer" pop-up that appears while you browse. This creates urgency and nudges users to make quicker decisions, which can lead to impulse buys. Another common nudge is the "you may also like" feature that suggests products after a selection is made. These recommendations tap into social proof, nudging consumers toward choices that seem popular or trendy, often leading them to spend more than they initially planned.

While the advantages of nudging can be significant, they also raise important ethical questions. Sometimes, the line between guidance and manipulation can become blurry, prompting us to consider the morality of nudges. Some critics argue that nudging can swing into paternalism, where those in power impose their values on others while claiming to promote well-being. For instance, while nudges aimed at encouraging healthier eating might be well-meaning, it's worth questioning whether individuals should have the autonomy to make their own choices, regardless of the outcomes. This creates a key tension: how can we balance providing support with respecting personal freedom?

Additionally, there's the issue of transparency. Often, people have no idea they are being nudged, leading to concerns about manipulation. If individuals don't recognize the subtle influences on their decision-making, can they truly say they are free to choose? The ethical aspects of nudging challenge us to think about our values and the broader effects these strategies may have. Are we genuinely enhancing decision-making, or are we unconsciously directing people down predetermined paths?

Despite these ethical challenges, the potential benefits of nudging are hard to ignore. When done thoughtfully, nudges can encourage healthier lifestyles, foster financial stability, and enhance overall well-being. The key is to implement these strategies carefully, ensuring they empower people rather than limit their choices. A considerate approach to nudging takes into account both the desired outcomes and the values of those being nudged, aiming to guide them toward decisions that truly reflect their interests.

Overall, the art of nudging serves as a powerful reminder of the unseen influences that shape our everyday choices. By appreciating how small changes in our environment can lead to significant shifts in behavior, we can become more aware of our decision-making processes. Whether we're navigating healthcare choices, making financial decisions, or shopping, recognizing these gentle prompts empowers us to take charge of our lives.

As we grow more aware of the nudges around us, we can navigate our choices more effectively and seize opportunities for growth. The next time you're faced with a decision—big or small—pause for a moment to consider the factors affecting your choice. Are you being nudged toward a path that aligns with your true values, or are you simply reacting to the clever design of your surroundings? By reflecting on these questions, you can develop a more intentional approach to decision-making and ensure that your choices genuinely represent who you are.

Environmental Influences: Physical Spaces vs. Digital Realms

The environment around us isn't just a backdrop; it plays a big role in shaping the choices we make every day. Whether we're stepping into a store or logging onto a website, we enter spaces designed to evoke certain feelings and reactions. The mix of physical and digital environments creates a complex web of influences that guide our decisions, often without us even realizing it.

When we think about shopping in a store, our senses come alive. Imagine the smell of fresh bread filling the air at the grocery store, the vibrant colors of fruits and veggies neatly arranged, or the soft tunes playing in the background. All these details are carefully planned to create a vibe that encourages us to spend money. Stores know that a pleasant shopping experience can keep us browsing longer, which usually leads to more sales. Shopping shifts from a chore to a delightful experience that tempts us instead of just meeting a basic need.

Take a moment to think about how grocery stores are set up. They often have specific paths designed to guide shoppers through the aisles in a particular order. Essentials like bread and milk are usually tucked away at the back, prompting customers to pass by tempting items before they reach what they originally came for. This clever strategy not only boosts the chances of impulse buys but also invites shoppers to linger and explore. Everything from the layout to the eye-catching signs and even the placement of checkout counters contributes to this carefully designed setup, nudging us toward certain behaviors.

On the other hand, the digital shopping world presents its own set of challenges and possibilities. Online shopping sites work hard to replicate the sensory experiences we get in stores, but they do this in different ways. For example, think about how websites are organized. They use a mix of visual tricks—like colorful banners, buttons, and pop-ups—to steer our attention toward particular products or deals. The aim is to create an easy and enjoyable experience. However, this can also lead to decision fatigue, where the sheer volume of choices feels overwhelming.

Online shopping platforms use algorithms to recommend items based on what we've bought or looked at before. While this makes the shopping experience feel more personalized, it can also feel a bit like being watched. Every click we make gets tracked and analyzed, allowing these platforms to refine their nudges even more. This raises important questions about privacy. Are we truly making our own choices, or are we just reacting to a clever web of suggestions designed to boost sales?

The issue of choice overload is particularly noticeable in online settings. When faced with too many options, we can find ourselves stuck, unable to decide amid a flood of possibilities. In physical stores, the selection is often more curated, making it easier to choose. However, scrolling endlessly through products online can lead to frustration and hasty decisions. Sometimes, this results in a quick exit from the site or, worse, a rushed purchase without really thinking it through.

Both physical and digital environments use psychological tricks to influence our choices. Take the decoy effect, for instance. In a store, having a pricier item nearby can make a moderately priced product seem like a steal, nudging us toward that option. Similarly, online shopping often showcases various price points, where a not-so-great option is placed next to a pricier item, encouraging us to choose what appears to be the best deal.

Another psychological principle at work in both settings is anchoring. When we see a price, it serves as a reference point for evaluating other options. If the first item we pick up in a store costs $50, anything cheaper will likely feel like a bargain. Online, this might show up as sale prices next to the original prices, creating a perception of savings that might not be as significant as it seems.

Looking at the differences between physical and digital spaces, it's clear that touching, smelling, or even tasting products in stores builds a stronger emotional connection to our shopping experience. These sensory interactions lead to a deeper engagement with the items we consider buying. In contrast, online shopping often lacks these sensory experiences and relies on visuals and descriptions to attract shoppers. This absence can leave us feeling less satisfied and disconnected from what we're purchasing.

Let's not forget the social aspect of shopping in physical spaces. The interactions we have with other customers or cashiers can foster a sense of community. These social connections often sway our choices, making us more inclined to buy items that seem popular or are recommended by others. Shopping online, while convenient, can feel isolating. Without those social cues, we miss out on the shared experience, leaving us to sift through choices alone.

The contrast between these two environments shows just how important it is to understand how each one affects our decision-making. Being aware of these dynamics can help us make choices that truly reflect our needs and values, rather than just reacting to the signals around us. By recognizing the psychological principles in play, we can navigate the complexities of both physical and digital shopping with a sharper eye.

As we become more aware of these influences, we can start to ask ourselves some important questions about our shopping habits. Are we genuinely in control of our purchases, or have we been subtly nudged toward choices that serve someone else's interests? How often do we make impulse buys based on our environment instead of taking a moment to think about what we really need?

The key to managing these influences is intentionality. By understanding how both our physical and digital environments shape our choices, we can approach decision-making more mindfully. Instead of letting outside factors dictate our preferences, we can take charge of our decisions and ensure they truly align with who we are.

The interplay between physical spaces and digital realms creates a rich landscape of factors that influence our choices. By grasping the unique traits of each environment, we can better navigate the complexities of choice architecture and become more thoughtful participants in our shopping journeys. Awareness empowers us to reclaim control over our decisions, allowing us to live in a way that reflects our true values and dreams. Happy shopping, and may your choices be as deliberate as they are fulfilling!

Faye Chandler

Chapter 2: Understanding Revealed Preferences

Defining Revealed Preferences: Desires and Motivations

Understanding revealed preferences is a fascinating look into how we make decisions. It's about uncovering the true desires and motivations that influence our choices in everyday life. Think of it like peeling an onion, where each layer reveals more about what we genuinely want versus what we say we want. At its core, revealed preferences show us that there can be a big difference between our words and our actions, shedding light on the hidden forces that drive us.

Take Sarah, for example. She's a bright-eyed aspiring artist who dreams of bringing her thoughts and feelings to life on canvas. She talks excitedly about her visions and the stories she wants to share through her art. But instead of pursuing her passion, she finds herself stuck in a corporate job, sitting at a desk and dealing with responsibilities that feel safe but also suffocating. Sarah's longing for a creative career is clear when she chats with friends, but her daily choices—sticking with her stable job—reveal a preference for security over the risks that come with chasing her artistic dreams.

Sarah's experience is not unusual; many people struggle with the tension between their dreams and the choices they end up making. As we navigate life, we often find ourselves at a crossroads where our values, past experiences, and societal pressures come into play. Each of these factors shapes our preferences, leading us to make decisions that may not resonate with our true selves.

Now, let's consider the powerful influence of society on our choices. We live in a world that often measures success by tangible things like wealth, job titles, and belongings. This pressure can make people feel like they need to chase these markers, sometimes at the cost of their true passions. For instance, a young professional might dream of a minimalist lifestyle but feel trapped in a cycle of accumulating things. They might talk about wanting simplicity and purpose, yet find themselves drawn into consumerism and the status it seems to bring.

The gap between what we say we want and the choices we actually make can be confusing. Our actions often speak louder than our words, revealing our true motivations. This isn't just a theoretical idea; it has real implications for how we understand ourselves. When we take the time to reflect on our choices, we can start to uncover what drives us. Maybe it's the fear of what others will think that keeps us in a conventional job instead of taking a leap into entrepreneurship. Or perhaps we believe that happiness comes from material wealth, which leads us to choose things over experiences.

To illustrate this, let's meet Tom. He's a mid-level manager in his thirties and often shares his desire to travel and explore new cultures. He paints beautiful pictures of adventure when he talks with friends. However, when vacation time comes, Tom usually opts for a staycation, prioritizing work and routine over exciting exploration. This behavior shows the disconnect between his desire for adventure and the choices he makes.

Tom's situation emphasizes a key truth: the motivations behind our decisions can be complicated and sometimes contradictory. He might genuinely want to travel, but his tendency to stick to his familiar routine highlights how comfort and safety can overshadow the desire to discover new things. Reflecting on Tom's story, we can ask ourselves how often we let fear or the comfort of routine guide our choices, keeping us from going after what we really want.

Next, let's look at Julia, who has always dreamed of being a writer. Yet, she finds herself locked into a corporate job that offers stability but lacks inspiration. Julia often shares her writing dreams with friends, talking about the novels she wants to create. But as the years go by, her writing gathers dust, and her artistic dreams remain unfulfilled. What's driving Julia's choices? It could be a fear of failure or a belief that her writing isn't good enough, keeping her stuck in her job. Her actions show a preference for security over the risk of pursuing her passion.

As we explore these stories, it's important to recognize the many factors that shape our revealed preferences. Our past experiences can heavily influence our motivations. For example, someone who grew up facing financial struggles might prioritize a stable job over pursuing creative ambitions, while another person with a supportive background might feel encouraged to chase their passions without hesitation. Everyone's story is unique, but they all share themes of desire, fear, and the influence of society.

Reflecting on these examples reveals that understanding our revealed preferences can help us make more genuine decisions. When we recognize what motivates our choices, we can challenge the norms around us and start taking steps to align our actions with our true values. While it might be uncomfortable to confront the gaps between what we say and what we actually do, this self-awareness is crucial for leading a more fulfilling and intentional life.

To really grasp how revealed preferences work, we should also think about the cultural expectations that complicate our decision-making. In many societies, there's heavy pressure to stick to certain paths, often dictated by tradition or the expectations of peers. This pressure can create a gap between what we truly want and the choices we make, resulting in decisions that reflect societal norms rather than our personal desires.

Consider how education and career choices are often viewed. Many cultures suggest that success comes from following a specific path—going to college, finding stable employment, and achieving financial success. People may feel obliged to follow this path even if their true interests lie elsewhere. Take the aspiring musician who feels pushed to earn a business degree; they might end up in a job that doesn't match their passions. This isn't just one person's story; it's a feeling many people experience.

Moreover, the way we talk about our desires matters too. The language we use can shape how we view our choices and what motivates them. When we frame our goals with "shoulds" rather than genuine wishes, we risk losing touch with what we really want. For example, saying, "I should start exercising," sounds more like an obligation than a desire. In contrast, saying, "I want to feel energized and healthy," comes from a place of true motivation. It's important to see how our words can influence our feelings and, ultimately, our choices.

As we begin to understand our own revealed preferences, we can adopt a more thoughtful approach to decision-making. By reflecting on our motivations, we can better grasp what we desire. This practice encourages us to dig deeper into our preferences, revealing our authentic selves. Regularly asking ourselves questions like "What do I really want?" or "What fears are guiding my choices?" can help us break free from societal pressures and lead us to make choices that align with our true values.

Embracing this journey of self-discovery reveals that our revealed preferences aren't fixed—they change as we grow and have new experiences. Our desires and motivations can shift, mirroring our evolving perspectives and life situations. Recognizing this fluidity is important because it allows us to adjust our choices to fit who we are becoming.

In summary, understanding revealed preferences offers a valuable way to explore our motivations and choices. By recognizing the gap between what we say we want and what we actually do, we can start to unpack the influences of society, fear, and personal values that shape our decisions. Reflecting on the stories of people like Sarah, Tom, and Julia reminds us how crucial it is to be true to ourselves in our choices. By practicing self-awareness and thoughtful reflection, we can navigate our preferences with more clarity and intention, leading to a more authentic and meaningful life. We have the power to shape our paths, creating a journey that truly resonates with who we are and what we aspire to achieve.

The Say–Do Gap: What We Claim vs. What We Do

In our everyday lives, we often stumble upon a puzzling truth: there can be a big difference between what we say we believe in and how we actually act. This clash, known as the say-do gap, raises important questions about the sincerity of our actions. At its core, this gap highlights the disconnect between our stated values—what we claim to care about—and the choices we make, which can sometimes be completely at odds with those values.

This disconnect is often tied to a feeling called cognitive dissonance, which describes the discomfort we face when our beliefs and actions don't match up. Picture someone who passionately promotes caring for the planet, sharing heartfelt messages on social media about environmental protection. Yet, when it comes to the temptation of trendy fast fashion, they find themselves making impulse buys, abandoning the very ideals they advocate for. This isn't just an individual struggle; it's a reflection of a larger pattern in human behavior and identity.

Let's take a closer look at Mark, a vibrant yoga instructor who loves sharing his passion for healthy living. He posts colorful plant-based recipes on Instagram, encouraging his followers with photos of fresh salads and smoothies. However, behind the scenes, Mark can't resist indulging in fast food during late-night study sessions, convincing himself it's a well-deserved treat after a tough day. His friends admire his healthy lifestyle, yet Mark feels trapped in a cycle of cravings that contradict his public image. This gap between his beliefs and actions perfectly illustrates the say-do gap, where the pressures of how we see ourselves and how society expects us to act collide.

Mark's experience isn't unique. It reflects a broader trend where many people profess commitments to ideals—like health, environmental protection, or social justice—while their everyday choices often tell a different story. This inconsistency can lead to feelings of guilt and confusion. Why do we say one thing and do another? This question digs deep into the complex layers of human psychology, revealing how social pressures and our sense of self influence our decisions.

Take Emma, for example, a devoted advocate for animal rights. She regularly participates in protests and volunteers at local shelters. Yet, despite her passionate efforts, she often finds herself drawn to the quick convenience of fast food, choosing meals that don't match her stated beliefs. The conflict Emma feels—a clash between her values and her behavior—leads to a cycle of guilt that only grows with each meal choice.

Emma's struggle is a common one. In a world that emphasizes convenience and instant gratification, many of us face the challenge of making choices that clash with our stated values. This ongoing battle between ease and ethics often leaves us questioning our own authenticity. It's important to recognize that these contradictions are not just personal failings; they come from deeper psychological roots intertwined with our sense of self and the cultural stories that shape our lives.

The impact of this say-do gap reaches far beyond personal feelings of guilt. It gives us a unique way to look at societal norms and expectations. When most people claim to value things like health, sustainability, or equality but collectively fail to act on those values, it raises questions about the authenticity of our culture. Are we just putting on a show, saying we believe in certain ideals without truly living them out?

Let's think about Jason, a high-powered executive who frequently talks about the importance of work-life balance. He often gives motivational speeches to his team about taking breaks and caring for mental health. Yet, despite his inspiring words, Jason often finds himself working late, sending emails at all hours, and skipping meals to meet tight deadlines. His actions starkly contrast with his professed values, creating a façade of balance that hides a reality of overwork and burnout.

Jason's situation underscores a crucial point: the societal pressure to appear successful can overshadow genuine self-care. In the workplace, there can be an unspoken expectation to always be available and productive, pushing individuals to act against their own stated values. This creates a significant gap between what we claim to prioritize and how we actually behave.

As we navigate these stories, it's important to encourage reflection on our own behaviors. Taking time to think deeply about our choices can help uncover the reasons behind our inconsistencies. By looking closely at our decisions, we can start to understand what influences us. Why do we sometimes choose convenience over our values? What fears or pressures from society shape our choices?

To help in this reflection, consider asking yourself some thought-provoking questions. Think about times when you've chosen a quick, unhealthy meal instead of sticking to your goal of eating well. What led to that decision? Was it a lack of time, a sudden craving, or maybe the comfort of familiar options? Reflecting on these moments can help you gain insight into your behaviors and the motivations behind them.

Closing the say-do gap requires a conscious effort and self-awareness. It's vital to pay attention to our choices, which helps us align our actions more closely with our values. By practicing self-reflection, we can work toward living authentically, moving beyond merely performing our values to genuinely embodying them.

Bridging this gap often involves making small, gradual changes that can lead to significant transformations over time. For instance, if you care about sustainability but find yourself buying fast fashion, consider approaching your wardrobe more intentionally. Look into sustainable brands, try shopping second-hand, or create a capsule wardrobe focused on quality instead of quantity. Each small decision can reinforce the values you hold dear.

Similarly, if health is a priority for you, think about making healthier choices easier. Try meal prepping or keeping nutritious snacks on hand so you're less tempted by unhealthy options when hunger strikes. By creating an environment that supports your values, you can slowly reduce the gap between what you say you believe and how you live your life.

Ultimately, the journey to close the say-do gap is a personal one, shaped by our unique experiences and aspirations. It calls for a commitment to self-discovery and the courage to face the discomfort that comes from our inconsistencies. Recognizing that our preferences can change as we grow offers a powerful chance for transformation.

As we engage in this process of aligning our actions with our beliefs, we not only nurture a more authentic self but also contribute to a culture that values integrity. When we act in ways that reflect our values, we inspire others to consider their own say-do gaps and the effects of their choices.

At its heart, the say-do gap goes beyond being just a personal issue; it reflects the complexities of human behavior and societal expectations. By looking at the stories of individuals like Mark, Emma, and Jason, we gain valuable insights into this multifaceted phenomenon. Each narrative reminds us that our choices are not just transactions; they are expressions of who we are. By engaging in thoughtful reflection and embracing the journey of self-awareness, we can start to close the gap between what we say we value and how we choose to live. This process has the potential to lead us toward a more intentional and fulfilling life, where our actions truly reflect our authentic selves.

Everyday Revelations: Impulse Buys and Habitual Patterns

Shopping often gets labeled as a boring chore, something we simply need to check off our list. However, it's so much more than that. It acts as a reflection of our deepest wishes, fears, and, importantly, our everyday habits. When we take a closer look at why we make impulse buys and why we tend to spend regularly, we enter a fascinating world where the desire for immediate pleasure can sometimes overshadow our long-term goals and values.

Imagine this: Sarah, a busy marketing executive, just wrapped up a tough week at work that pushed her to her limits. As she heads home on a Friday evening, the stress from looming deadlines and the weight of her responsibilities hang over her like a cloud. What could make her feel better? A quick stop at her favorite mall. With her mind swirling in exhaustion and her heart craving a little joy, Sarah can't resist the bright, shiny sale sign calling to her from the store window. "50% off everything!" it shouts, as if it knows exactly what she needs.

Walking inside, Sarah is hit by a wave of sensations: bright colors, the lovely smell of new clothes, and the warm smiles of the sales staff. Each item feels like it promises a little happiness, a little joy, and, most importantly, a way to escape the weight of her workweek. As Sarah picks up a trendy pair of shoes, a rush of excitement sweeps over her. This is her way of treating herself, a small indulgence that lifts her spirits, at least for a moment.

But as the weekend winds down, that initial thrill gives way to a nagging feeling. Did she really need those shoes? Was that fleeting joy worth the hit to her bank account? The answer, as is often the case, is tangled in the mix of psychology and behavioral economics. The pull of instant satisfaction can cloud good decision-making, leaving Sarah—and many others—wondering about the choices they make when driven by their emotions.

Impulse buying is more than just a lack of willpower; it's closely tied to our feelings and the signals in our environment that guide our shopping habits. Marketers know this well and create spaces filled with sights and sounds that spark feelings of happiness and satisfaction. We, as shoppers, often find ourselves caught up in this cycle, where each purchase becomes a temporary escape from stress and the everyday grind.

Let's look at another example. Tom is a college student juggling classes and a part-time job—a tough balancing act that often leads him to the brink of burnout. One evening, feeling overwhelmed by upcoming exams, Tom decides to treat himself with a little retail therapy. He steps into an electronics store, where the latest gaming console calls to him like a lighthouse in a sea of stress. "It's just a little treat," he tells himself, convincing himself that the console will help him unwind after long nights of studying. But as he walks out with the console, guilt creeps in. Does he really need this distraction, especially with bills piling up?

Tom's experience sheds light on the connection between impulse buys and emotional triggers. The excitement of escaping reality through material items often clouds our thinking, making it easy to lose sight of what we truly need and the goals we want to achieve. This behavior can become a habit, forming a cycle that's hard to break.

The places we shop play a huge role in shaping these habits. Retailers are experts at designing environments that encourage spending. Bright lights, eye-catching displays, and even specially chosen music create a setting that invites shoppers to linger and buy more. Our shopping choices often adapt to these environments, leading us to make decisions that might not align with who we really are.

But what if we turned our attention inward? What can we learn from our shopping habits? Realizing when we use shopping as a way to cope is a crucial first step. The stories of Sarah and Tom remind us of the importance of being aware of our feelings. By recognizing our emotional triggers, we can start to tell the difference between what we genuinely need and what we just want in the moment.

Now let's pivot from impulse buys to habitual patterns, which also tell an important story in our lives. Habits form the foundation of our daily choices, influencing the routines that shape who we are. However, we should ask ourselves if these habits truly reflect our values or if they are just leftovers from what society expects of us.

Take Rachel, for example. She is a fitness enthusiast who sticks to a daily workout routine every morning. Initially, this habit was a way to boost her health and feel good. Yet over time, it transformed into a strict obligation that left no space for flexibility. On some days, Rachel feels utterly exhausted, but she pushes herself to work out, worrying that skipping a session would mean she's not dedicated enough. What started as a choice aligned with her values has turned into a source of stress, distancing her from the very passion that sparked her journey.

Rachel's story encourages us to think about our own habits. Are our routines helping us grow and feel fulfilled, or are they just conforming to what we think we should do? By examining our behaviors, we may find that some habits no longer serve us. Perhaps it's that daily coffee run we do out of obligation rather than real desire, or the need to attend social events that drain us instead of lifting us up.

Practicing mindfulness is a powerful way to create a better connection between our choices and our values. By developing an awareness habit, we can start to identify our triggers—both emotional and environmental. This practice encourages us to pause before making decisions, allowing us to reflect on whether our choices truly resonate with who we are. For example, instead of automatically adding items to our online shopping cart, we might ask ourselves: "Do I really need this? Will it add to my happiness? Is there a better way to spend my time or money?"

Alongside mindfulness, practical strategies can help us create a more thoughtful shopping experience. Setting specific spending goals can be effective. For instance, instead of wandering the aisles aimlessly, you might create a monthly budget for fun purchases and stick to it. This approach encourages you to be more mindful about where your money goes.

Another useful strategy is to declutter your shopping environment. If certain stores or websites always tempt you into impulse buys, consider steering clear of them or limiting your visits. By shaping your shopping experiences, you can actively change the patterns that impact your decisions.

Embracing a minimalist mindset can also help clarify our shopping habits. By prioritizing quality over quantity, we can shift our focus away from seeking instant satisfaction and toward investing in items that truly enhance our lives. This approach prompts us to pause and think about what really matters, leading to more intentional choices.

As we navigate through consumer culture, it's important to remember that shopping is not just about transactions—it reflects our deeper values and dreams. By examining our impulse buys and habits, we can gain valuable insights into who we really are. The stories of Sarah, Tom, and Rachel illustrate how easy it is to fall into mindless shopping, but they also show us the possibility for change.

In this journey toward being our true selves, self-awareness lights the way. By recognizing our triggers, practicing mindfulness, and putting practical ideas into action, we can align our choices with our values, creating a life that truly reflects who we are.

Shopping can become a path to self-discovery, encouraging us to think about our wants and motivations. Each purchase is an opportunity to look inward, prompting us to tackle the deeper questions that shape our lives. Are we seeking comfort, connection, or approval? Do our choices empower us, or do they leave us feeling hollow?

Ultimately, the secret to understanding impulse buys and habits is to know ourselves better. As we embrace self-awareness and mindfulness, we can break the cycle of mindless consumption and build a lifestyle that encourages us to make thoughtful choices. The road to authenticity might not always be clear, but each step brings us closer to aligning our choices with who we really are. By engaging in this journey, we not only change how we view shopping but also nurture a life that aligns with our most heartfelt values and dreams.

Chapter 3: The Psychology of Choice

Cognitive Biases: Anchoring and Loss Aversion

Picture yourself at a car dealership, surrounded by the fresh smell of new upholstery and the sparkle of shiny vehicles under bright lights. You've done your homework, figured out your budget, and you're all set to make a decision. You spot a car that checks all your boxes: it's reliable, fuel-efficient, and that deep blue color just grabs your attention. But then, you catch a glimpse of the price tag, and suddenly, everything revolves around that one number. That initial price becomes your anchor—the reference point for all your future choices.

Anchoring is a psychological trick where we rely too much on the first piece of information we come across. In this scenario, the sticker price of the car you're eyeing sets the standard against which you judge other options. Even if you look at different models or makes, that first price keeps influencing your thoughts. You might discover another car that's technically better, with more features at a lower price, yet because your mind is still stuck on that original anchor, the new choice feels less enticing.

Marketers know all about this little quirk of ours. Just think about it: a dealership advertises a car for $30,000, but then they put up a sign announcing a $5,000 discount. Suddenly, that new price of $25,000 looks like a bargain, even if the car's actual value hasn't changed. This tactic works because it plays on our habit of getting fixated on that first number, allowing our ability to think logically to fade under the weight of our emotions.

In everyday life, we encounter anchors everywhere—from the prices we see while shopping to the time estimates we get for tasks. A famous experiment demonstrated this when participants were asked to estimate the percentage of African nations that are United Nations members. Their answers shifted dramatically based on a random number they had seen before answering. This "random" number acted as an anchor, showing just how easily we can be swayed by seemingly irrelevant information.

Whether we're choosing a place to eat or deciding on a new job, anchoring can shape our views in ways that might not be obvious at first. Take picking a restaurant, for example. You look at a menu and see the most expensive dish priced at $50. When you finally choose the $25 entrée, it feels reasonable compared to the $50 option, even if a similar meal down the street costs only

$15. That anchor can trick you into spending more just because you fixated on the higher price.

Now, let's switch gears and talk about another psychological phenomenon that influences our choices: loss aversion. We humans tend to feel the sting of losing something much more intensely than the joy of gaining something. This isn't just a theory; it's a well-established fact in behavioral economics. A classic example of this is the "Asian disease problem," which shows how people's decisions can be swayed by the fear of loss rather than the possibility of gain.

In the study, participants faced two options during a hypothetical disease outbreak threatening 600 people. They could pick between two programs to tackle the disease. Program A would save 200 lives, while Program B offered a 33% chance to save all 600 people but a 66% chance that no one would be saved. When presented this way, most people preferred the sure thing (Program A).

However, when the same options were framed in terms of deaths, everything flipped. They now had Program C, which would result in 400 deaths, versus Program D, which had a 33% chance that no one would die and a 66% chance of 600 deaths. This time, driven by the urge to avoid loss, participants chose Program D, highlighting how the way we present choices can greatly affect decision-making.

The discomfort of potential losses often overshadows the satisfaction we might feel from equivalent gains. This can lead us to make choices that aren't really in our best interest, simply because we want to protect ourselves from perceived threats. The fear of losing something can cloud our judgment about future options and opportunities.

For example, think about someone who's hesitant to leave a stable but unfulfilling job for a potentially exciting new position. The familiarity of their current job serves as an anchor, while the fear of losing that security makes them overlook the positive possibilities. The excitement of what could be takes a backseat to the fear of the unknown. This trepidation can affect relationships and investments, where the fear of loss keeps us clinging to what we know, even if it's not the best choice for us.

So how do we start to untangle these cognitive biases from our decision-making? The first step is to recognize them. When we understand that these biases exist, we can begin to question the anchors that hold us back and the losses that loom larger than gains in our minds. Being aware is empowering; it helps us take a step back and look at our choices with a more thoughtful eye.

One helpful way to counteract the effects of anchoring is to actively look for more information. Instead of settling for the first price we see or the first opinion we get, we can expand our research and gather a range of viewpoints. This approach can lessen the influence of that initial anchor and lead us to choices that truly reflect our values and needs.

When it comes to dealing with the fear of loss, changing our perspective can be key. Rather than fixating on what we might lose, let's think about what we might gain. Focusing on the potential benefits instead of worrying about losses can help us embrace change rather than shy away from it. For instance, envision the job opportunity not just as leaving a current position, but as opening doors to new skills, connections, and experiences.

Another useful strategy is to create a decision-making framework that weighs the pros and cons. By writing down potential outcomes—both positive and negative—we can better grasp the full range of consequences related to our choices. This can lessen the emotional weight that loss aversion has on our decision-making and help us see things more clearly.

As we navigate through the tricky waters of decision-making, it becomes clear that understanding these cognitive biases isn't just a theoretical exercise; it's a crucial part of personal growth. By recognizing the anchors that hold us back and acknowledging the fear of loss that shapes our choices, we can take control of our decisions.

In the end, the journey toward making thoughtful choices invites us to be more aware of the psychological influences at play. It encourages us to look deeper and examine the motivations behind our preferences. As we work to dismantle the biases that hinder us, we can take brave steps forward, aligning our choices with who we truly are and creating a more fulfilling life. Each decision becomes more than just a reaction to what's happening around us; it's an opportunity for growth and intention—a chance to build a life that truly reflects our dreams.

Emotion-Driven Decisions: The Role of Feelings

Imagine yourself in a lively café, the delicious aroma of your favorite coffee filling the air as you pause to decide what to have for breakfast. You scan the menu, and your eyes are immediately drawn to fluffy pancakes topped with warm maple syrup and fresh berries. Your stomach lets out a little growl, but then a nagging thought creeps in, suggesting that maybe you should choose the avocado toast instead—after all, it's healthier, and you've been trying to make better choices lately.

In this everyday moment, you find yourself at a crossroads, where your emotions and logic are in a bit of a tug-of-war. The pancakes stand for indulgence and happiness, while the avocado toast represents self-control and health. As the seconds tick by, the pull of the pancakes becomes stronger, and before you know it, your heart has made the decision for you, leaving reason behind. You order the pancakes, delighting in that comforting feeling.

This little scenario is a snapshot of a much bigger truth: our emotions have a huge impact on the decisions we make, often overshadowing our logical thinking. Emotions aren't just background noise; they shape our choices. They affect how we see things, raise the stakes, and even turn simple decisions into meaningful moments.

Think about the often tricky choice of picking a career. Many people feel torn between chasing their passions and settling for a more stable, well-paying job. Picture someone who absolutely loves art but feels pushed to pursue a career in finance due to societal expectations. As they weigh their options, emotions enter the picture. The joy of creating art lights up a spark of happiness that a corporate job just can't match. On the other hand, the fear of not having enough money looms large, casting a shadow over their dreams. In the end, this emotional back-and-forth can lead to a decision that reflects their feelings more than a cold, hard look at the pros and cons.

Research in psychology shines a light on how emotions guide our decision-making. For example, studies show that feeling good can really boost our creativity and problem-solving skills. When people are in a positive mood, they're more likely to think outside the box and come up with creative solutions. But when negative emotions take over, we might find ourselves making hasty decisions driven by fear, anxiety, or regret.

Consider the case of an investor facing a tough financial decision. They often ride an emotional rollercoaster as they watch stock prices shift. In moments of panic, an investor might sell shares at a loss, driven by fear of further decline. Yet during euphoric moments, they might hold onto stocks longer than they should, convinced their value will keep climbing. Both situations show how emotions can lead to choices that stray from a smart investment strategy.

Taking a moment to reflect on our emotions can be an enlightening practice. It encourages us to look closely at how our feelings—whether good or bad—shape our choices. One helpful tip is to keep a decision journal. When you face a choice, write down not just the pros and cons but also the emotions you're feeling. Are you excited, anxious, or maybe feeling torn? This simple act of acknowledging your feelings can bring clarity and help you distinguish between emotional urges and logical reasoning.

As we explore this connection between emotions and decision-making, it's crucial to understand the importance of emotional intelligence. By paying attention to our feelings, we can better understand what drives us. Knowing why a particular choice makes us feel a certain way gives us the power to navigate our decisions with more awareness. For example, if you discover that your desire for a specific job comes from a fear of missing out rather than genuine interest, you can reevaluate your priorities and make a more thoughtful choice.

Moreover, being aware of our emotions can improve our relationships. When we recognize how our feelings influence our decisions, we can better empathize with others and express our needs. Imagine a friend feeling neglected because you often prioritize work over spending time together. By realizing that your decision to work late is rooted in a fear of falling behind rather than a lack of care for the friendship, you can approach the situation with honesty and openness. This clarity not only helps you make kinder choices but also strengthens your bonds with others.

In the world of decision-making, balancing emotional instincts with rational thought is key. Emotions can guide us powerfully, but unchecked feelings can mislead us too. To find that balance, think about creating a decision-making framework that respects both feelings and logic.

For example, when you're facing a big decision, create a two-column chart. On one side, list the emotional factors—joy, excitement, fear, and so on. On the other side, write down the logical considerations—potential outcomes, risks, and benefits. By visually outlining both aspects, you gain a clearer understanding of your decision, helping you weigh your options more effectively.

Incorporating mindfulness practices into your daily routine can also help manage emotional influences. Taking a few moments to breathe deeply and center yourself before making a decision can provide clarity and calm, allowing you to approach choices with a clear mind. Activities like meditation, journaling, or simply taking a stroll can help you process your emotions and lead to more thoughtful decision-making.

Ultimately, the journey of making decisions isn't just about the choices themselves; it's about understanding the emotions that drive them. This awareness encourages us to explore our values, desires, and the deeper motivations that shape our preferences. Each decision becomes more than just a single choice; it reflects who we are as individuals.

So the next time you find yourself at a crossroads—whether it's choosing breakfast, picking a career, or even deciding on a relationship—take a moment to check in with your emotions. Let yourself feel, but don't forget to think. By blending your feelings with logical thought, you can make choices that truly align with your authentic self. As you walk this path of emotional awareness, decision-making shifts from a daunting task to a thoughtful practice—one that resonates with your genuine desires and leads to a more fulfilling life.

In a world full of choices, we have the power to navigate our paths. When we acknowledge the role of emotions in our decisions, we learn to use our feelings as tools rather than obstacles. This journey of self-discovery opens doors to a richer, more intentional life, allowing us to create lives that reflect our deepest aspirations. After all, every choice we make, no matter how small, is a step toward becoming the person we aspire to be.

The Paradox of Choice: Freedom or Overwhelm?

Freedom often shines as a symbol of modern life. We're told that having choices empowers us, steering us toward lives filled with happiness and fulfillment. Whether it's picking out a breakfast cereal from an aisle crammed with colorful boxes or deciding which movie to watch on a streaming service packed with thousands of titles, we cling to the belief that choice equals freedom. But, as the saying goes, "with great power comes great responsibility," and that's where the problem comes in—the paradox of choice.

Picture yourself standing in front of an expansive wall of ice cream flavors at your favorite shop. Sure, you have the classic options like vanilla and chocolate, but what about that rich tiramisu? And then there's a zesty lemon sorbet and even an exotic lavender-infused treat! As you weigh whether to stick with your favorite Rocky Road or venture into something new, excitement begins to blend with anxiety. What should be a simple pleasure can quickly turn into a confusing dilemma. You might feel the pressure as the person behind you grows impatient, adding to the stress of making the perfect choice.

This scenario captures a typical experience in today's world of choices. Barry Schwartz, a behavioral economist and author of "The Paradox of Choice: Why More Is Less," emphasizes that while having options can enhance our freedom and independence, too many choices can lead to feeling stuck and unhappy. Schwartz's research reveals a surprising truth: when faced with an overwhelming number of options, we often struggle to make any decision at all. The fear of regret looms large, creating a psychological load that can dim any joy we might find in the choice.

Now, think about shopping for a new pair of jeans. In the past, you might have had just a few styles and brands to consider. Today, you face a dizzying array of choices: skinny, bootcut, high-waisted, distressed, and a lineup of washes that could make your head spin. As you browse through the options, what started as excitement can quickly turn into confusion. You may find yourself thinking, "What if I pick the wrong style? What if I miss out on the perfect fit?" With more choices, you might start questioning your taste, your preferences, and even your worth. Ultimately, you could leave the store empty-handed, feeling defeated rather than empowered.

This feeling of buyer's remorse isn't just a minor hassle; it's tied to the way we make decisions. When we face too many choices, we can end up spending far too long analyzing our options, weighing the pros and cons, and second-guessing ourselves. The outcome? Anxiety and dissatisfaction, often paired with a longing for simpler times when decisions were easier.

According to Schwartz, the paradox of choice isn't merely about how many options we have; it's also about their quality. An abundance of choices can lead to less satisfaction with our decisions because we often hold ourselves to impossible standards. With so many options available, we may feel pressured to find the "perfect" fit, the ultimate experience, or the best product. This quest for perfection can chip away at our confidence and leave us feeling perpetually unsatisfied, turning the act of choosing into a source of stress instead of joy.

Think about your last big purchase—maybe a new phone. You do your research, read reviews, and compare features. Once you finally pick a model, you're suddenly faced with more choices: color, storage capacity, accessories, and even service plans. After diving deep into comparisons, the excitement of getting your new device can be dimmed by the nagging thought: "Did I really choose the best one?" This situation can transform what should be a thrilling moment into a lingering worry about whether you made the right choice.

Our expectations can make things even more overwhelming. With every choice comes the chance for regret, and when we are surrounded by so many options, the fear of making the wrong one feels magnified. Schwartz suggests that when we choose from a limited selection, we can feel satisfied because justifying our decisions is easier. But when we're bombarded with choices, every decision carries the heavy question: "What if there was something better?" This mindset can lead to a persistent sense of dissatisfaction, turning decision-making into an emotional battleground.

To help ease the stress of having too many choices, we can adopt strategies that bring clarity and simplicity. One effective method is to set decision criteria before diving into options. This means figuring out what truly matters to you before you start shopping. For example, when looking for jeans, you might decide on comfort, price, and style as your key factors. By narrowing your focus, you make the decision process smoother and lessen the anxiety of facing countless possibilities.

Practicing mindfulness can also significantly reduce the stress that comes with making choices. Taking a moment to breathe and reflect on your values and priorities allows you to slow down instead of rushing through the decision-making process. By creating space for thoughtful reflection, you can cut through the noise of outside expectations and reconnect with your true preferences.

It's also possible to unlearn perfectionism, which often heightens the pressure of making choices. Adopting an attitude of "good enough" can help you navigate decisions more comfortably. When you find yourself stuck in the search for perfection, remind yourself that no choice has to be perfect. Instead of chasing the ideal outcome, value the learning process that comes with making a choice. Every decision you make, regardless of its results, is a step in your growth and understanding.

Reflecting on your experiences with choice can be a powerful tool, too. Noticing times when you felt overwhelmed can shed light on your decision-making patterns. Maybe you realize that certain types of choices—like those related to social events—often cause you more anxiety. Recognizing these patterns can help you identify triggers and develop personalized strategies to manage them.

Additionally, sharing the weight of your decisions with friends and family can provide a support network that lightens the load. Talking through your options can offer fresh perspectives and let you hear the experiences of others. This exchange can remind you that you're not alone in feeling overwhelmed, and it can empower you to make choices that align with your values.

As you navigate the complexities of decision-making in a world filled with options, it's helpful to remember that choice doesn't guarantee happiness. Instead, fulfillment comes from how intentional you are with your choices. By sharpening your awareness and putting strategies in place to handle the stress of decision-making, you can take back your sense of control and create a more satisfying experience.

Let's not forget that life is a series of choices, often reflecting our deepest dreams and values. Each choice presents a chance for growth, learning, and self-discovery. The next time you find yourself staring at an overwhelming array of options, pause for a moment, take a deep breath, and think it through. Embrace the freedom that comes with choice, but also remember that it's perfectly fine to let go of the quest for perfection.

Ultimately, navigating the paradox of choice is about developing a thoughtful relationship with your decisions. By setting clear intentions and allowing yourself the grace to choose imperfectly, you open the door to a more fulfilling and meaningful life. In a world where choices seem endless, it's the clarity of your intentions that will guide you through the maze of options and help you make decisions that truly resonate with who you are. After all, the real power of choice lies not in how many options we have but in our ability to recognize what aligns with our values and dreams, paving the way for a more satisfying journey through life.

Chapter 4: Cultural Influences and Social Norms

Cultural Backgrounds and Their Impact on Preference

The world is like a beautiful quilt, woven together by countless cultures, each adding its own unique pattern to the fabric of our human experience. As we go through our daily lives, we often see things through the eyes of our cultural backgrounds. These backgrounds shape who we are, influencing our tastes, decisions, and the paths we choose. These influences can act like subtle waves, guiding us in ways we might not notice until we take a moment to think about them. Understanding these cultural influences can help us uncover the reasons behind our choices and allow us to make decisions that truly reflect who we are.

Our cultural backgrounds come from a mix of factors such as where we live, the traditions we follow, the values our families teach us, our religious beliefs, and the historical events that have shaped our communities. All of these elements help form the stories we tell ourselves about the world. For example, someone who grows up in a community-focused culture may value family and teamwork more than personal success, while someone from a culture that celebrates individuality might prioritize personal achievements and independence. These differing values can lead to various preferences that affect everything from career decisions to how we spend our money.

Think about two friends, Sarah and Omar, who grew up in very different places. Sarah was raised in a lively city, where ambition and competition were part of everyday life. From an early age, she was encouraged to pursue her dreams and strive to stand out. In contrast, Omar grew up in a quiet village where tradition and community were emphasized. His upbringing taught him the importance of family and the impact of his choices on those around him. So, when Sarah and Omar face important decisions in their adult lives—like choosing a job, buying a house, or even picking a restaurant—they do so from their own unique cultural viewpoints.

These differences in how we make choices can also extend to how we view social norms. Take success, for example. In many Western cultures, especially in North America, success is often measured by personal achievements—like climbing the corporate ladder, earning a lot of money, and showcasing individual accomplishments. On the other hand, many Eastern cultures may define success by family honor, collective well-being, or contributions to society. These varying definitions can significantly influence decisions, affecting everything from career paths to shopping habits, as people navigate the expectations laid down by their cultural backgrounds.

Education is a great place to see these cultural influences in action. In cultures that value academic excellence, students may feel intense pressure to excel on standardized tests, sometimes at the expense of discovering their passions or developing well-rounded skills. This pressure can lead them to prioritize grades over what truly interests them. In contrast, in cultures that encourage a more holistic approach, students might explore a variety of fields, such as the arts, sports, and community service, resulting in preferences that are more in line with their authentic selves.

Cultural influences are not fixed; they change over time and with context. As our world becomes more interconnected, many people find themselves balancing multiple cultural influences. For example, a young professional from India moving to the fast-paced environment of Silicon Valley may feel torn between the high expectations of their family and the individualism celebrated in their new home. This clash of cultures can lead to an interesting mix of preferences as they learn to balance their traditional values with the modern ideas around them.

The rise of social media has added another layer of complexity to how our cultural backgrounds affect our choices. With platforms that quickly share ideas and values across borders, we see a digital culture that can sometimes overshadow local traditions. Crafting an online persona can lead people to adopt interests that don't completely match their real lives. For instance, a teenager might feel the need to buy the trendiest clothes not because they align with their style but to fit into an ideal image created by social media influencers. This can lead to choices that, while trendy, might leave them feeling disconnected from who they really are.

The desire for social acceptance is a powerful force shaping our preferences. As we navigate our choices within our cultural backgrounds, wanting to fit in can often lead to decisions driven by the fear of being left out rather than true desire. This is especially clear in consumer behavior, where trends spread quickly, pushing people to keep up with the latest fads. The pressure to conform can create a cycle of consumption where looking authentic becomes more important than being truly authentic.

Real-life stories illustrate how these cultural influences play out. For example,

Maria grew up in a family that valued sustainable living. Because her family was mindful of the environment, she developed a strong preference for eco-friendly products. However, when she went to university, she found herself surrounded by friends who didn't care about sustainability. Wanting to fit in, Maria started buying fast fashion items that clashed with her values. This struggle shows the conflict between one's upbringing and the need for social acceptance, highlighting how societal norms can sometimes push individuals away from their true preferences.

Another compelling idea is cultural nostalgia, where people feel a pull towards their roots. As globalization blurs cultural lines, individuals may find themselves rekindling their connection to their traditions and values, seeking authenticity in a rapidly changing world. This renewed interest in cultural heritage can show up in many ways, from an appreciation for traditional foods and rituals to a revival of art forms. These preferences highlight how adaptable cultural influences can be, as individuals redefine their identities based on their experiences.

The relationship between cultural backgrounds and social norms encourages us to think deeply about the nature of our preferences. Are they genuinely ours, or are they shaped by outside influences? As we make decisions, it's important to take a step back and reflect on how our backgrounds affect our choices. By thoughtfully examining these influences, we can work towards a life that truly reflects our values and aspirations.

Ultimately, understanding the roots of our preferences is more than just an academic exercise; it's a path to empowerment. Recognizing the cultural currents that shape our choices helps us navigate the complexities of decision-making with greater understanding. As we cultivate this awareness, we create opportunities to make choices that genuinely resonate with who we are—choices that reflect our values, respect our cultural backgrounds, and ultimately lead to more fulfilling lives. The landscape of our preferences is vast and intricate, shaped by countless influences that surround us. Embracing this complexity is not only freeing; it's also a crucial step toward living authentically in a world full of choices.

Social Validation: Peer Pressure and Consumer Choices

In life, few forces have a stronger impact on us than social validation. It plays a huge role in the decisions we make, shaping how we view our needs and desires. Often, it nudges us along paths we might not have chosen if we were on our own. To truly grasp this idea, we have to face the complex nature of being human: we want to be our own person, yet we also crave acceptance from others. Peer pressure, whether it's loud and obvious or soft and subtle, acts like a guide, steering us toward what's considered acceptable or desirable in our social circles.

Imagine peer pressure as a gentle voice in a bustling room, encouraging us to go along with the crowd. It can show up in clear ways—like a friend insisting you try that new trendy restaurant—but it can also sneak in through unspoken expectations that linger in the air. At its heart, peer pressure taps into our deep need to belong. This desire is rooted in our history; humans are social beings, and our survival often depended on fitting into groups. So, when we conform to our friends' norms, we often feel safe, accepted, and sometimes even admired.

Picture a familiar scene with a group of friends deciding where to eat. Six friends come together on a Friday night, each with their unique tastes. As they chat about dinner options, Alex gets excited about a new sushi spot that's all the rage on Instagram. Meanwhile, Jamie secretly longs for a comforting Italian meal at their local pizzeria, but he finds himself nodding along with Alex, swept up in the sushi excitement. The thought of being the odd one out weighs heavily on him.

In this situation, Jamie's choice is largely influenced by the desire for social approval. The need to fit in overshadows what he truly wants. Even though he knows the pizzeria has the best lasagna in town, the fear of causing awkwardness among friends makes him go along with the group. This scenario highlights how social validation can shape our consumer choices, pushing us to align with what others expect rather than what we personally desire.

These moments go beyond just where to eat; they seep into the larger world of consumerism, where brands become symbols of status. The latest smartphone, designer handbag, or fashion trend can transform into badges of acceptance. When a new gadget launches, it's not just another tool—it's a statement about where you fit in socially. The attraction to these products often comes more from the validation they promise than from their actual usefulness.

Take a college campus where a new sneaker brand creates a buzz. Students rush to buy the latest limited edition, not just for comfort or style, but to share in the collective excitement. The desire to fit in can spark a frenzy of purchases, with many lining up to grab a pair. Behind every smile in selfies lies an internal question: "Would I have chosen these shoes if my friends weren't raving about them?"

Social validation also thrives online, where social media has amplified peer pressure in ways we never imagined. Platforms like Instagram and TikTok have created an environment where likes, shares, and comments serve as new forms of acceptance, quickly setting trends and shaping preferences.

In this digital age, the pressure to create an enviable online image often leads people to make consumer choices based more on popularity than on what truly resonates with them. It's common for someone to buy the latest fashion item, not out of love for it, but because they've seen countless influencers showcase it. This cycle can trap individuals in a loop of consumption that values appearance over genuine self-expression.

The beauty industry illustrates this trend perfectly, with makeup styles that can change overnight. A look that gets thousands of likes one week can be completely out of style just days later. The pressure to keep up with ever-changing standards can be overwhelming, especially for young consumers who feel they must constantly adjust their choices to fit in online.

Consider Mia, a teenager who, inspired by her social media feed, wants to mirror the perfection shown by her favorite influencers. She spends hours scrolling through their posts, taking note of every product they promote. When her friends suggest a shopping trip, the pressure intensifies—Mia feels she must embody the aspirational lifestyle she sees online. What seems like a harmless quest for beauty hides a deeper conflict: Mia struggles between appreciating her natural beauty and chasing an idealized image shaped by outside opinions.

At this point, it's crucial to recognize the potential downsides of social validation. The relentless quest for acceptance can lead to consumer choices that clash with personal values, resulting in feelings of guilt, dissatisfaction, or regret. When personal preferences are overshadowed by the need to fit in, it stifles individuality and blocks true self-expression.

Yet, there is a way to navigate this challenging landscape and turn peer pressure and social validation into sources of strength. The first step is to be mindful of our choices and develop an awareness of what drives our decisions. By questioning whether our choices reflect our values or come from outside pressures, we can regain control over our decisions.

For instance, when choosing what to wear, instead of automatically grabbing the latest trend, we can pause and think about what truly makes us feel good. Is it the comfort of our favorite jeans, or the flashy outfit that promises acceptance? Taking the time to reflect on our preferences helps us make choices that are true to ourselves.

Additionally, building a supportive community that values individuality can greatly lessen the impact of peer pressure. By surrounding ourselves with friends who appreciate authenticity, we create an environment where personal choices are honored rather than judged. This change can transform the urge to conform into a movement toward being true to ourselves, where diverse preferences are celebrated.

Another way to resist peer pressure is to understand that "social rejection" can be a valid choice. It's easy to think acceptance requires fitting in, but true freedom comes from realizing that our uniqueness fosters genuine connections. Embracing our personal preferences—even when they differ from what's popular—can lead to meaningful self-discovery and growth.

The world of consumer choices is vast and complicated, shaped by social validation, peer pressure, and individual desires. Each decision we make reflects who we are, and understanding the influences can help us navigate this complex landscape more intentionally. By recognizing the balance between external validation and our internal desires, we can carve a path that truly reflects our authentic selves.

Ultimately, it's about finding a middle ground between wanting to fit in and being true to ourselves. The journey toward making authentic choices isn't just about pushing back against peer pressure—it's about redefining our relationship with it. By practicing mindfulness, embracing our uniqueness, and nurturing supportive communities, we can take back control against social validation. The choices we make can then be a celebration of who we are, rather than a reflection of who we think we should be. In this beautiful dance of life, the goal is to find our unique rhythm and move to the beat of our own drum.

Identity Formation: The Role of Social Media

In a world where technology is everywhere, the internet has become an essential part of our daily lives. It connects us like never before and allows us to interact in countless ways. Social media isn't just a place to share photos and updates anymore; it has turned into a stage for people to shape their identities and connect with others. Our digital identity isn't just a reflection of who we are; it's often carefully designed to meet the expectations of our online followers. The journey of forming our identity in this space is tricky, filled with how we see ourselves, how we're influenced, and how we seek validation from others.

At the core of our digital identity is personal branding. Just like businesses create their brands to attract customers, people use social media to craft images that appeal to their audience. This branding highlights certain traits, interests, or lifestyles, influencing how others see them. For instance, someone might display their adventurous side through travel photos or show off their cooking skills with pictures of fancy meals. What we choose to share—and what we decide to keep private—becomes a thoughtful strategy aimed at building an attractive online persona.

Take the stories of two friends, Sam and Alex. Both love to travel, but their social media profiles tell very different stories. Sam treats his feed like a highlight reel, picking out stunning images from beautiful places and thrilling adventures, often paired with inspiring quotes that make people dream of travel. His followers see him as someone who leads an exciting and spontaneous life. In contrast, Alex takes a more down-to-earth approach, sharing not just breathtaking views but also the everyday moments of his trips—like missed flights, overpriced hotels, and moments of homesickness. While his posts may not get as many likes or shares, they resonate deeply with those who appreciate genuine experiences over polished perfection.

This difference in how they present themselves shows how social media can stir up feelings of comparison and competition. Many users feel the pressure to keep up appearances, leading them to create a digital identity that aligns with what is popular or expected. It can be overwhelming to conform to the standards set by influencers and trends. This pressure creates what we call social comparison, where individuals measure their lives against the carefully crafted images of others. The fallout from this comparison can be significant; many people end up feeling inadequate or dissatisfied with their own lives.

Influencer culture plays a huge role in shaping these experiences. Influencers are often seen as trendsetters, with their lifestyles and opinions viewed as something to aspire to. They have a lot of sway over what people want to buy and how they think. Brands have caught on, and many partner with influencers to promote their products. This creates a win-

win situation where influencers gain sponsorships, and brands reach the audience they want in a more relatable way.

Just one post from a well-known influencer can greatly impact what people decide to buy. For instance, if a popular beauty influencer shares a new skincare line, it can lead to a spike in sales as fans believe that buying those products will improve their own lives in some way. This is not just true for beauty; it spans fashion, travel, fitness, and lifestyle. The power of influencer marketing has completely changed how brands connect with consumers, moving away from traditional ads to more personal endorsements.

The effects of this influencer-driven consumerism can be seen in the story of Jamie, a young woman who became fascinated by a lifestyle influencer's posts. The influencer painted a picture of a flawless life—amazing vacations, perfect skin, and a stunning wardrobe. Believing that buying the promoted products would help her achieve a similar lifestyle, Jamie started purchasing items she had never considered before, from high-end skincare products to designer bags. But when she looked into her closet, she felt a sense of emptiness. The beautiful items didn't bring the happiness and fulfillment she had hoped for.

This situation shines a light on a critical aspect of identity formation through social media: the risk of disillusionment. Carefully curated online personas create a false narrative that can lead people to chase after shallow markers of success and happiness. When real life doesn't match up to these idealized images, it can leave individuals feeling inadequate and disappointed.

The psychological effects of social media on identity formation can be deep, contributing to heightened anxiety and depression, especially among young people. Concepts like FOMO—fear of missing out— and the highlight reel phenomenon add to this sense of dissatisfaction. FOMO pushes individuals to engage in activities just to avoid feeling left out, often making them prioritize social interactions over what they truly want. It's as if every post serves as a reminder of what they might be missing, creating a cycle of desire and discontent.

At the same time, the highlight reel phenomenon emphasizes the gap between online portrayals and reality. As people scroll through their feeds, they may see their friends' lives as glamorous and exciting, leading to a skewed perception of reality. In a world where comparison is the norm, personal achievements can seem insignificant next to what others put out there. It's easy to forget that social media is often a polished version of reality, a collection of moments that rarely shows the full picture of life's ups and downs.

Navigating this complicated landscape takes thoughtfulness and an understanding of what truly matters to us. Being true to oneself is so important in a world that often values image over substance. Taking the time to reflect on personal preferences and desires can help individuals make choices that resonate with who they really are instead of just succumbing to outside pressures.

To build a healthier relationship with social media, there are several strategies that can be helpful. First, it's key to intentionally curate your own social media feed. Following accounts that uplift and inspire, rather than those that spark comparison and discontent, can create a digital space that fosters real connection and support. Engaging with content that aligns with your values and interests can strengthen your identity and create a sense of belonging rooted in authenticity.

Additionally, focusing on face-to-face interactions and experiences can lead to a deeper sense of fulfillment. Spending time with friends and family in person can create meaningful connections that are often lost online. These moments can remind us of who we truly are, free from the filters and expectations of social media.

Encouraging a culture of authenticity is also vital. By inviting friends and family to share their genuine experiences—both the highs and the lows—we can break down the illusion of perfection that often fills social media. Normalizing vulnerability and openness can help create a supportive community that values realness over appearance.

Ultimately, building a healthier relationship with social media and forming our identities comes down to recognizing that we have choices. Every person has the power to define their identity on their own terms, free from societal pressures or the trends set by influencers. Celebrating one's uniqueness and personal preferences can lead to a more authentic and satisfying life.

As we navigate the challenges of forming our identities in the digital age, it becomes clear that social media is not just a tool for connection; it shapes our identities in many ways—sometimes in ways we don't even realize. By approaching these platforms thoughtfully and purposefully, we can take back control of our stories and align our choices with who we really are, paving the way for a more genuine life amidst the hustle and bustle of the digital landscape.

Chapter 5: The Power of Defaults

Understanding Defaults: A Hidden Force in Decision-Making

In a world filled with choices, the word "default" carries a lot more weight than it seems. It often acts like a quiet guide, steering us through our decision-making processes without us even realizing it. So, what does "default" really mean? Simply put, a default is the option that's automatically selected if we don't make an active choice. It's the preset that kicks in unless we decide to change it. This simple idea lies at the core of many decisions we face each day, influencing everything from our health to our finances.

Let's picture a young professional named Sarah. Like many of her friends, she's often bombarded with decisions: what to eat, how much to save for retirement, and how to communicate with her healthcare provider. One day, she learns that her employer has a retirement savings plan. To her surprise, she finds out that if she doesn't do anything, a part of her paycheck will be automatically deducted and put into the plan. In this case, the default is clear: she can either opt in without lifting a finger or go through the hassle of actively opting out.

Sarah's experience reflects a broader trend in our society, where defaults are often set by companies, governments, and other organizations that shape the environments we live in. A choice that seems simple can actually lead us down a path that affects our financial stability and future well-being. The power of defaults lies in their subtlety; we often don't realize how much they influence our choices until we start to see the effects.

In the realm of healthcare, for example, defaults can greatly impact organ donation. Several countries have an opt-out system, where citizens are assumed to be organ donors unless they say otherwise. This is quite different from the opt-in model, which requires individuals to take action to become donors. The results of these systems are striking. In countries with opt-out policies, organ donation rates soar, saving countless lives, while in places with opt-in systems, many potential donors remain unutilized simply because they didn't take the extra step to enroll. This is a powerful example of how defaults can shape societal norms and health outcomes without individuals even realizing it.

The influence of defaults becomes even clearer when we think about our online behavior. Recall the last time you signed up for an online service. Most platforms set defaults that automatically subscribe users to newsletters or enroll them in data-sharing agreements. Often, we just click 'accept' without reading the details, handing over our personal information and preferences to companies that might not always have our best interests at heart. This results in a cascade of decisions made for us, showcasing the hidden yet powerful role of defaults in our digital lives.

Let's also consider the role of defaults in technology. Take a look at your smartphone—each app comes with preset options that determine how it functions. Whether it's notifications, privacy settings, or even the layout of your home screen, these defaults help shape your experience with technology. Have you ever felt overwhelmed by the number of notifications you get? This is often due to the default settings that come pre-installed. You can change them, of course, but many people simply go with the defaults, resigning themselves to a digital life crafted by someone else's choices.

Defaults aren't just products of technology and policy; they are woven into the very fabric of our society. They tap into the human tendency to resist change; we often stick with what we know rather than exerting the mental energy to make a different decision. This can lead to a sense of complacency, where individuals float through life, shaped by choices they didn't actively make.

However, it's worth noting that defaults can be harnessed for good. Thoughtfully set defaults can nudge people towards better choices. Consider a school cafeteria that places fruits and vegetables at the front of the line while putting less healthy options further back. Kids are more likely to grab the healthier items, not because they made a conscious choice, but because they've been gently guided by the layout. This simple strategy can encourage healthier eating habits among children—a crucial goal in a time when childhood obesity is on the rise.

The idea of defaults also ties into behavioral economics, which looks at how psychological aspects influence our economic choices. A key concept in behavioral economics is that the way choices are presented can significantly impact our decisions. Researchers Daniel Kahneman and Amos Tversky studied this idea, showing that people often rely on mental shortcuts, or heuristics, to simplify decision-making. When faced with complex choices, our brains naturally lean toward the default option because it requires less cognitive effort.

This phenomenon has major implications for policymakers and organizations. By understanding the impact of defaults, they can create environments that encourage better choices among the public. The "nudge" theory, proposed by Richard Thaler and Cass Sunstein, promotes using these insights to design policies that enhance public welfare while still allowing freedom of choice. By establishing default options that lead to positive results, we can empower individuals to live healthier, more secure lives.

As we move through life's endless decisions, being aware of the defaults around us is key. They might seem trivial, but their effects can be significant. Next time you face a choice, take a moment to think about the defaults in play. Are they working in your favor, or are they leading you somewhere you didn't intend to go? By fostering this awareness, we can start to take control of our decision-making, making sure that the choices we make align with our true values and goals.

The real power of defaults is their ability to influence our lives in ways we often overlook. They shape our decisions, influence our behaviors, and ultimately guide our futures. By recognizing the hidden forces at work in our daily lives, we can learn to use the power of defaults for our advantage. Whether it's setting up a retirement savings plan, choosing healthier eating options, or managing personal technology settings, being able to spot and change the defaults in our lives is a skill that can lead to greater clarity and intentionality.

Ultimately, the challenge is straightforward: engage with defaults consciously, deciding whether to accept them or adjust them to fit your values and priorities. It's about becoming active participants in our decision-making instead of passive receivers of choices made for us. By understanding defaults better, we can empower ourselves to make decisions that truly reflect our desires and dreams, paving the way for a more intentional and fulfilling life.

Beneficial Defaults: Healthier Lifestyles and Financial Gains

In our busy lives, the vast number of choices we face can sometimes feel overwhelming, making it hard to make good decisions. That's where the idea of defaults comes in, providing a simple and effective way to help us. Picture yourself walking into a cozy restaurant, filled with delicious smells and a long list of menu items. After a long day, you're hungry and maybe a little stressed. As you look at the menu, all you really want is to make a choice quickly. But what if, instead of having to choose, the restaurant had already picked a healthier option for you? What if the default choice was a yummy salad instead of greasy fries? This isn't just a nice idea; it's a real way to improve our health and finances when defaults are set up to help us.

Let's look at a real-life example that shows how this works: a hospital that wanted to promote better health for its patients and staff decided to change its default menu. Instead of the usual high-calorie, low-nutrition foods, they focused on healthier options. This small change had a big impact. Patients, who might have reached for fries or sugary drinks out of habit, started choosing salads and whole grains because those were the default options. Hospital staff also began making better food choices during their breaks. Not only did the health of patients improve, but the workplace culture got better, too. Conversations shifted to wellness, and staff members began adopting healthier lifestyles outside of the hospital.

This shows the magic of beneficial defaults—simple changes that lead to big improvements. By making nutritious food the default, the hospital didn't just adjust a menu; it helped people make better choices without thinking too much about it. Having a default option can lighten the mental load, allowing individuals to embrace healthier habits more easily.

But the influence of defaults isn't just about what we eat; it reaches into our financial lives as well. Automatic enrollment in retirement savings plans is a great example. Think about a young couple, the Johnsons, who are busy juggling work, kids, and adult responsibilities. They know saving for retirement is important, but they've never gotten around to setting it up. When their employer introduced automatic enrollment, everything changed. With a simple default that directed part of their paycheck into a retirement fund unless they opted out, they found themselves on a path to financial security they never imagined.

At first, the Johnsons were surprised by the deductions in their paychecks, but soon they began to see the benefits. They were saving without even thinking about it. It felt easy, almost like a gift they didn't know they needed. Over the years, they watched their savings grow, along with their confidence about the future. They started to understand the importance of planning ahead, all because of a default option that gently nudged them in the right direction.

Research backs up the idea of beneficial defaults. A study by the National Bureau of Economic Research found that organizations with automatic enrollment see participation rates jump—often by 30 to 50 percent—compared to traditional methods where individuals have to actively sign up. This shows us how powerful default choices can be. People tend to stick with what they know, and when that default is an automatic enrollment in a savings plan, they are more likely to build wealth over time without having to make active decisions.

Defaults, then, aren't just choices; they're powerful tools that shape our behaviors in ways we don't always notice. They can spark positive changes, especially when designed thoughtfully to promote health and financial well-being. The potential here is huge, touching areas like public policy, business responsibility, and personal health. When organizations realize how effective defaults can be, they can create environments that inspire better choices.

We can apply the idea of healthy defaults not just in hospitals but also in schools, workplaces, and communities. For example, imagine a local school cafeteria that places fruits and vegetables at the front of the line, while less healthy options are pushed to the back. Kids are more likely to grab the healthier foods—not necessarily because they chose to, but because they've been subtly guided by the setup. This simple move can help kids develop healthier eating habits, giving them tools for a lifetime of well-being.

The idea of beneficial defaults comes from behavioral economics, which looks at how our thoughts influence our choices.

Researchers like Daniel Kahneman and Amos Tversky have explored the biases that often affect our decisions. Their work shows that people like to conserve mental energy and usually gravitate toward the easiest options available. Defaults often serve as shortcuts, making it easier for us to follow a path of least resistance.

As we think about defaults, it's clear they're not just about efficiency; they're about empowerment. By recognizing the defaults in our lives and advocating for better options when needed, we can take charge of our health and financial futures. It's essential to realize that the choices we face aren't always straightforward. Sometimes, the most important decisions are the ones we don't actively make at all.

So, the next time you find yourself feeling stuck with choices—whether at the grocery store, in a restaurant, or while planning your future—take a moment to think about the defaults at play. Are they helping you, or leading you in the wrong direction? By being aware of these preset choices, you can start to engage with them thoughtfully, making changes to align with your values and goals.

Ultimately, the strength of beneficial defaults lies in their ability to guide us toward healthier lifestyles and better financial outcomes, often without us having to think about it. They can reshape our surroundings, steering us toward choices that support our well-being in a subtle yet powerful way. As we navigate our complicated world, it's these defaults that will quietly help us lead healthier, more secure lives. The journey to harnessing this power begins with awareness and engagement, transforming the defaults we encounter into chances for growth, health, and financial success.

Personalizing Defaults for Better Decision Outcomes

There's something really intriguing about how our daily choices connect with the settings that shape them—what psychologists and behavioral economists call "defaults." We've seen how smart defaults can boost our health and financial well-being, but the real magic kicks in when we take control and tailor these defaults to match our values and goals. Imagine stepping into a world where you're not just going through the motions of making choices, but actively crafting your own decision-making journey.

This is exactly where the power of personalized defaults shines bright. When we take the time to shape our surroundings, we set defaults that reflect our dreams and aspirations. Think of it as tuning an orchestra so that every note played aligns beautifully with the song we want to create in our lives. From our eating habits to exercise routines, financial choices, and time management, we can adjust our default settings to encourage outcomes that truly benefit us.

Let's take a look at nutrition. In a world full of fast food and convenience often overshadowing quality, the challenge is finding a way to develop healthy eating habits. One effective way is to personalize our defaults in the kitchen. Consider stocking your fridge and pantry in a way that makes healthier options the easy choice. Instead of letting chips and sugary snacks be the first thing you see, why not fill your kitchen with colorful fruits and vegetables, ready to go? When healthy choices are the most accessible, they become the defaults that guide you toward a more nourishing diet.

Think about Mark, a busy professional who, like many, felt swept up in the hectic pace of work and life, relying heavily on takeout and quick snacks. One day, he discovered meal prepping—an approach that could make healthy cooking his default behavior. Mark set aside a few hours each weekend to prepare nutritious meals, storing them in convenient containers. This small change completely transformed his relationship with food. Instead of feeling overwhelmed by what to eat after a long workday, he simply reached for his prepped meals without a second thought. Now, the default was a home-cooked, healthy option. Over time, he not only lost weight but also felt more energetic and happier.

This story brings home a crucial point: by taking time to create personalized defaults in our nutrition, we empower ourselves to make choices that align with our health goals. Making these changes is relatively simple and often just requires a little bit of planning. As we look deeper into this topic, we'll uncover strategies across different areas of life where personalizing defaults can lead to incredible results.

Now, let's turn our focus to exercise. How many of us have found ourselves caught in the cycle of excitement and burnout when trying to stick to a new workout program? The initial allure of a gym membership can fade quickly when life gets busy. But here's the good news: by personalizing defaults in our fitness routines, we can build a consistent exercise habit without relying solely on willpower.

Think about pre-scheduling workout classes or blocking out time in your calendar for physical activity. This simple shift turns a potentially tough decision into a regular part of your life. For example, if you sign up for a fitness class that happens at the same time every week and set a reminder on your phone, you're creating a default that makes it easier to prioritize your health. Just imagine waking up on a Tuesday morning, knowing your spin class is waiting for you. The commitment is already made, and your default is set—you just show up.

There are many inspiring stories of people who have successfully woven exercise into their lives using these strategies. Take Sarah, a single mom balancing a demanding job and her kids' busy schedules. At first, she struggled to carve out time for exercise and often felt guilty for wanting a break. After some thinking, she decided to transform her mornings into dedicated "me time." By waking up an hour earlier and committing to a virtual workout class she could do from home, Sarah found that this adjustment significantly improved her health and happiness. Exercise was no longer an option—it became a must-do part of her daily routine.

When it comes to finances, personalizing defaults can be just as impactful. For instance, automatic savings plans have shown that when saving for retirement is the default, people are much more likely to participate. But what if we went even further? People can set up their bank accounts to automatically transfer a portion of their paycheck into a savings account as soon as they get paid. This automatic transfer sets a default that aligns with the goal of building wealth.

Let's consider the Smith family, who were eager to save for their two children's education. They noticed that when all their funds were in one account, it was all too tempting to overspend. Their solution? They opened a separate savings account just for education expenses and set up an automatic transfer that deducted a set amount from their main account every month. The moment their paycheck came in, the money for savings was already out of sight, so they didn't have to think about it. This simple change shifted their perspective—saving became a natural part of their financial routine, rather than an afterthought.

The beauty of personalizing defaults is that it reaches beyond food, fitness, and finances; it seeps into how we manage our time, too. In our increasingly busy lives, making thoughtful choices about how we spend our time can feel overwhelming. But by creating defaults around our schedules, we can take back control and ensure that we focus on what truly matters.

For example, think about blocking out time on your calendar for focused work. By setting aside specific hours for deep work or important tasks, you create a default that helps you avoid distractions. When colleagues and friends know you're unavailable during those hours, they're less likely to interrupt you with minor issues. This simple act of personalizing your time defaults can lead to greater productivity and job satisfaction.

Let's look at Lisa, a project manager with a never-ending to-do list. She often felt swamped, bouncing from one task to another without making real progress. After realizing she needed a change, Lisa decided to implement "focus blocks" in her daily routine. She reserved two hours each morning for uninterrupted work, during which she silenced her phone, closed her email, and focused solely on her most pressing projects. With this new default in place, Lisa found herself not just more productive, but also more engaged and fulfilled in her job.

As we explore these different areas, it's important to understand that personalizing defaults gives us the power to navigate our decision-making processes intentionally. It's about creating an environment that nudges us toward the behaviors we want to cultivate. This approach can apply to many aspects of life, from improving sleep hygiene to enhancing social interactions.

For instance, if you're looking to cut down on screen time before bed, you might decide to leave your phone on the other side of the room at night, making it a bit less convenient to scroll endlessly. What used to be a default behavior—binge-watching shows or scrolling through social media—can shift into the default of picking up a book instead.

The stories of people like Mark, Sarah, the Smiths, and Lisa remind us of the potential within each of us. They show that we don't have to be victims of our circumstances. Each one of us has the ability, through thoughtful design, to create an environment that supports our dreams.

As you think about your own life, reflect on the defaults that shape your decisions. Are they leading you to where you want to go? If not, how can you start personalizing them? Begin small; maybe today you can decide to drink a glass of water first thing in the morning or schedule a weekly family night to strengthen your connections.

The journey of personalizing defaults isn't just about changing habits; it's about reclaiming control over our lives. It's about making choices that resonate with our values and dreams while navigating a world often designed to push us toward less beneficial options.

By understanding the power of defaults, we can use their influence to create a life that reflects what we truly want. This is what empowerment looks like—taking charge of our environments and shaping the defaults that guide our choices. It's an invitation to engage with our lives, making decisions that fit who we are and who we want to become.

As Alice's story illustrated earlier, being aware of how defaults work can be a game-changer. By stepping back and examining the choices around us, we gain insight into our habits. Realizing that we can actively design our surroundings is incredibly freeing.

Imagine walking through life with a heightened awareness, able to recognize the defaults at play. Every moment becomes a chance to engage thoughtfully with our choices. We become not just participants but curators of our own lives, crafting paths that lead to healthier, more satisfying outcomes.

So, as you think about the choices you face, ask yourself: What defaults can you personalize to help you achieve your goals? Which of your current habits can you tweak to better align with your values? The answers often lie within the small, steady changes we make every day. Over time, these choices can come together to build a life that feels intentional and authentic—a life guided by the defaults we set for ourselves.

Ultimately, the power of personalized defaults can transform the way we approach decision-making. It's not just about choosing a salad over fries or saving a part of our paycheck; it's about creating a life where our choices truly reflect our desires and dreams. By taking control of our defaults, we pave the way for a more intentional and fulfilling life, one choice at a time.

Faye Chandler

Chapter 6: Identifying and Recalibrating Your Preferences

Reflective Exercises: Identifying True Values

Imagine standing on the edge of a vast ocean, feeling the cool spray of the waves as they crash rhythmically against the shore. Each wave symbolizes a decision or choice we make in our day-to-day lives. Yet, beneath the surface, there are deeper currents—the true values that guide us. These values act like a compass, helping us navigate the sea of choices we face every day. To sail through these waters with confidence, we need to explore the depths of our core values. This journey of self-discovery isn't just a brief dive into our thoughts; it's a thrilling adventure that, while personal, can bring incredible insights.

Reflective exercises are great tools for this exploration, acting like a map and a guide. You might wonder, "Why should I take the time for this? Can't I just go along with what everyone else does?" The thing is, while it can be easier to follow the crowd, doing so often means sacrificing our authenticity. We may find ourselves chasing after what's popular or expected, only to end up feeling lost and unfulfilled. By identifying our true values, we can take back control over our lives, ensuring that our choices come from within rather than simply reflecting societal pressures.

To kick-start this journey, let's look at some reflective exercises that will help peel back the layers of superficial desires to reveal the real values underneath. A wonderful place to start is journaling. This can be a powerful way to reflect on yourself. Try to set aside a few quiet moments each day to jot down your thoughts. What experiences brought you joy? What moments left you feeling dissatisfied? Ask yourself thought-provoking questions like, "What am I willing to stand up for?" or "What do I want my legacy to be?" Let your thoughts flow freely, without any judgment. Writing creates a conversation with yourself, shining a light on the values that truly matter.

Another helpful technique is visualization. Imagine a day in your life where you feel genuinely fulfilled—what does that day look like? Who are you with? What activities fill your time? This isn't just daydreaming; it's a chance to picture a life that aligns with your values. Pay attention to the details; feel the emotions, hear the sounds, and see the sights. Once you've painted this vivid picture, take a moment to reflect on the values present in that scenario. Perhaps you value creativity, community, or adventure.

Whatever it may be, this vision can guide you toward living a more authentic life.

As we dig deeper, let's look at the idea of identifying peak moments in our lives. Think back to times when you felt energized, confident, or really content. These peak experiences often hold clues to our core values. For instance, a thrilling hike could highlight a love for exploration and adventure, while a day spent volunteering might reveal your commitment to service and community. Write down these peak moments and see what common threads run through them. This exercise not only uncovers your values but also helps you understand how they show up in your everyday life.

In our quest for self-discovery, stories of transformation can inspire and reassure us. Take the story of Emma, a corporate attorney who felt swept up in the whirlwind of her high-powered career. On the outside, she seemed to have it all—a hefty paycheck and a respected status. But deep down, Emma struggled with an emptiness that gnawed at her spirit. When she finally found the courage to try reflective exercises, she uncovered her true values: creativity and connection—both of which had been stifled in her corporate routine. With this newfound clarity, she shifted to a career in art therapy, where she now helps others express themselves through creativity. Emma's journey shows us how identifying our core values can lead to powerful changes, ultimately allowing us to live more authentically.

To enhance your journey, consider talking with trusted friends or family. Ask them what they believe your values are based on their observations. Sometimes, the people closest to us can spot patterns and values that we might overlook ourselves. This conversation can be eye-opening, helping you see strengths and values that may have been hidden under layers of self-doubt or societal expectations.

Throughout this reflective process, it's important to treat yourself with kindness. Self-discovery isn't a race; it's a gradual unfolding. Some values might surprise you, while others may feel familiar. There are no right or wrong answers; this is a personal journey, and each person's path will look different. By allowing yourself the space to explore, you can unlock profound insights.

As you reflect, remember to consider the societal influences that shape your values. From a young age, we're bombarded with messages about success, happiness, and fulfillment, which can lead us to adopt external standards as our own. Recognizing these influences helps us sift through the noise and identify what truly resonates with us.

Reflect on how your values align with societal expectations. Are you pursuing a career because you're passionate about it, or is it just seen as prestigious? Are you nurturing certain relationships out of genuine love or out of obligation?

Identifying our true values can serve as a powerful antidote to the chaos of the world. It brings clarity to a confusing landscape, enabling us to make choices that reflect our authentic selves. With this awareness, we can approach life with intention, aligning our actions with our core principles.

As you engage in these reflective exercises, keep in mind that the process of identifying your true values is a continual journey. Life is ever-changing, and as you grow, so will your values. Embrace this dynamic process, allowing yourself to develop and adapt as you uncover more about who you are at your core.

In time, you'll discover that your decisions reflect your authentic self, leading to greater fulfillment and a sense of purpose. While the ocean of choices may still seem vast and unpredictable, with your compass of true values firmly in hand, you can navigate those waves with confidence and grace.

Strategies for Recalibration: Aligning with the True Self

Now that the fog of self-reflection has lifted, revealing the bright colors of your core values, it's time to switch gears from understanding to action. This next step is all about recalibration—a process that helps you connect your daily choices and long-term goals with your genuine self. Think of recalibration like resetting your GPS; you've figured out where you want to go, and now it's time to chart the best route to get there.

One powerful tool to guide you on this journey is setting intentions. Imagine setting an intention as a way to clearly express what you want in life. When you set an intention, you're not just dreaming; you're outlining a path for your life and putting your energy behind it. A fun and effective way to solidify your intentions is to create an "Intention Board." This artistic collage isn't just a pile of images and words; it's a visual reminder of your dreams and serves as a daily nudge to help you live authentically.

To make your Intention Board, gather materials that resonate with your values. Look for magazines to cut out pictures that reflect your dreams—maybe a peaceful beach for your desire to relax or some bright art that symbolizes your love for creativity. Add in quotes that inspire you or affirmations that lift you up. The process of crafting this board can be uplifting and empowering, turning your abstract ideas into real visuals. Hang your board where you'll see it often—maybe above your desk or next to your bed. Let it shine as a guiding light for your thoughts, actions, and decisions.

While setting intentions is a great start to aligning with your true self, the next step is to create SMART goals. This handy framework makes sure your dreams don't just stay wishes but can actually become achievable plans. Each letter in SMART stands for Specific, Measurable, Achievable, Relevant, and Time-bound. This organized approach encourages you to break down your intentions into smaller, practical steps that you can realistically take.

For example, let's say you recognize that health is a key value for you, but it hasn't been a priority. Instead of saying, "I want to be healthier," which is a bit vague, you could create a SMART goal: "I will exercise for 30 minutes, three times a week for the next two months." This goal is specific (exercise), measurable (30 minutes), achievable (reasonable frequency), relevant (linked to your health value), and time-bound (a two-month commitment). By laying out such clear steps, you create a roadmap to guide you toward your goals, making it feel less overwhelming and more achievable.

But remember, setting intentions and goals is just the beginning. To keep the energy flowing on your recalibration journey, staying accountable is key. Getting a friend or mentor involved can make a huge difference. By sharing your goals, you create a sense of community and support, which helps you celebrate the wins and tackle any bumps along the way.

Think about the impact of a simple check-in. Whether it's a quick text or a coffee chat, having someone who knows your intentions can give you the push you need to stay focused. Take John, for instance. He wanted to pick up painting again after years away from it, so he shared his goals with his friend Lisa. They decided to meet every two weeks to talk about their creative projects, providing each other with encouragement and helpful feedback. This kind of accountability not only reignited John's passion for art but also strengthened his friendship with Lisa, creating a shared space for growth and inspiration.

Accountability can also come from tracking your progress. Keeping a journal or using an app to record your achievements can turn your intentions into measurable results. For example, if you set a goal to practice mindfulness for ten minutes each day, writing down your practice can help you see your progress over time, which reinforces your commitment to your intention. And looking back at your journey can remind you how far you've come, serving as a strong motivator during tough times.

Stories have a remarkable ability to illustrate the recalibration journey. Take a moment to consider the inspiring story of Sarah, who felt stuck in a corporate job that didn't excite her. Through self-reflection, she discovered her core value of freedom, which had been held back by her demanding career. With fresh clarity about what she wanted in life, Sarah created an Intention Board filled with images of travel destinations, quotes about adventure, and symbols of her lifelong dreams.

She set a SMART goal to save a specific amount of money each month for a year, so she could take a break to explore the world. Alongside her mother, who also loved to travel, Sarah regularly shared her goals, which kept her motivated and on track. Each month, they celebrated small victories together, like researching new places or planning their trips.

When the time finally came for Sarah's journey, her heart was full of excitement and anticipation. She set off on an adventure through Southeast Asia, discovering stunning landscapes and diving into vibrant cultures. This trip wasn't just a getaway; it was a reclaiming of her true self—a real embodiment of her alignment with her values. When Sarah returned from her travels, she not only brought back wonderful memories but also a renewed sense of purpose and vision that pushed her forward in her career.

Stories like Sarah's remind us how much of a difference recalibrating our values can make in our lives. They show that recalibration isn't just a one-time deal; it's an ongoing journey that grows and evolves as we do. Each step you take, every intention you set, and all the goals you achieve add up to a richer, more authentic life.

As you take on this journey, don't forget to celebrate your achievements—no matter their size. Whether you've completed a week of regular exercise or simply found time to meditate, recognizing your progress helps strengthen your commitment to recalibration. Surround yourself with positivity and people who lift you up; this supportive environment can significantly boost your motivation.

However, recalibration isn't always easy. The world is full of societal pressures that can lead us to question our choices or drift away from our intended path. It's so easy to get caught up in the expectations from family, friends, or social media. That's why it's crucial to take a moment to revisit your values and intentions from time to time. When you face outside pressures, grounding yourself in your core principles acts like an anchor, reminding you why your recalibration matters.

Think about times when societal pressures influenced your decisions. Have you ever chosen a career just because it seemed prestigious? Or felt pushed to live a particular lifestyle that didn't truly fit you? Recognizing these influences empowers you to take back control and make choices that reflect who you are.

Creating space for self-compassion is just as important. It's completely normal to face challenges along the way, and it's vital to remember that growth isn't always a straight line. Allow yourself the kindness to stumble and learn from setbacks; these experiences can teach you so much. Every time you recalibrate your values and align them with your true self, you build up your resilience and commitment to being authentic.

In a world that often tries to shape our preferences, recalibrating is a brave act—a statement that we are the builders of our own lives. With intention-setting as your compass, SMART goals as your roadmap, and accountability as your guiding star, you can navigate life's twists and turns while staying true to your core values. As you take this journey of alignment, remember that the most important relationship you'll ever nurture is the one with yourself. Embrace it, trust it, and let it guide you to the life that truly reflects the unique and vibrant person you are.

Navigating Societal Pressures: Staying True to Personal Choices

In the beautiful play of life, we often find ourselves assigned to roles that society thinks we should play. The costumes we wear—crafted from expectations, norms, and pressures—can feel heavy and confining. As you step onto this stage, equipped with the insights from your journey toward self-awareness, you might realize that the script wasn't meant for you at all. So, how do you handle the societal pressures that try to steer you off your path when all you truly want is to stay true to yourself?

In a world that loves comparisons, the rise of social media has made it easy to feel like we're falling short. Each scroll through our feeds brings images of seemingly perfect lives—friends landing promotions, coworkers sharing dream vacations, and influencers portraying flawless lifestyles. This constant measuring can chip away at our self-esteem and cloud our judgment, making it tempting to make choices based on what others find acceptable, rather than what truly speaks to us.

Take Emily, for instance. She was a shining star in her own right, filled with a passion for dance that ignited her spirit. But as she neared college, the chorus of voices from family, friends, and society began to overshadow her inner song. "You should choose a stable career, something respectable," they urged. "Think about your future!" The pressure mounted like an unyielding drumbeat, pushing her toward a conventional business degree instead of pursuing her love for dance.

Emily's experience is all too common, highlighting how social comparison can twist our values. When we succumb to these outside influences, we risk losing sight of who we are and what we genuinely desire. The real challenge is learning how to establish boundaries that safeguard our true selves.

Setting boundaries isn't just about saying "no"; it's about creating a safe space for your values to thrive. Start by identifying the areas in your life where you feel the strain of societal expectations. Are there particular conversations or situations that trigger feelings of inadequacy? Maybe it's during family gatherings when your career choices become a hot topic, or when you're scrolling through social media and feel the urge to keep up appearances.

Once you recognize these triggers, practice asserting your boundaries. It can help to communicate your choices clearly with friends and family. Not everyone will understand your journey, and that's perfectly fine. The goal is to cultivate an environment where open conversations can happen. For example, if someone questions your decision to follow a less conventional career path, seize the chance to share your passion and the reasons behind your choices. "I really believe that pursuing dance lets me express myself and brings me joy. I know it's not the usual choice, but it feels right for me."

Being open about your choices can ease tension and foster understanding. You might even inspire those around you to look at their own values and decisions in a new light. Honest dialogue can transform relationships from critical to supportive, creating a nurturing atmosphere for everyone involved.

Sometimes, conversations can become tricky. Practicing role-playing scenarios can be an effective way to prepare for these potentially awkward interactions. Imagine a situation where someone questions your lifestyle choices, or a family member expresses disappointment in your career path. How would you respond? Running through these conversations in your mind can give you the confidence to assert your viewpoint while still being respectful and understanding.

Consider a scenario where you're at a family dinner, and your uncle asks, "So, when are you going to get a real job?" Instead of feeling defensive or trapped, you could reply with something like, "I appreciate your concern, but I'm really passionate about my work in the arts. It fuels my creativity and lets me be my true self." By preparing for these moments and practicing your responses, you'll feel more equipped to maintain your authenticity, even when faced with societal pressures.

The stories of others who have faced similar challenges can light the way on your own journey. After wrestling with her family's expectations, Emily took a courageous leap. She enrolled in a dance academy, a choice that was both thrilling and nerve-wracking. To her delight, her passion bloomed, and her relationship with her family began to shift. Over time, they witnessed the joy dance brought her and started cheering her on, realizing that her happiness mattered most.

Emily's journey illustrates the beauty of staying true to oneself despite societal pressures. It shows that embracing your authenticity can inspire others to do the same.

When you honor your choices, you become a beacon of hope for those around you, proving that it's perfectly okay to chase passions that don't fit the mold.

Navigating societal pressures isn't just about resisting conformity; it's about celebrating the unique path of your life. This journey involves recognizing that while others may have opinions, they don't define your worth or shape your future. A crucial part of this process is showing yourself compassion. Embracing your choices and being true to who you are requires kindness toward yourself. Remember, it's okay to prioritize your values, even if they differ from the majority.

When doubts creep in, take a moment for self-reflection. Ask yourself, "What truly matters to me?" and "Am I making this choice for myself, or am I giving in to outside expectations?" This kind of introspection can ground you, reminding you of your mission to stay aligned with your true self.

Building a supportive network is another key strategy for maintaining your authenticity amid societal pressures. Surround yourself with people who uplift and inspire you—those who celebrate your choices, no matter how unconventional. Seek out communities that resonate with your values and dreams. Whether it's a group of fellow creatives, a circle of supportive friends, or even online forums, these connections can create a nurturing environment that strengthens your resolve to be yourself.

Shared experiences can be truly transformative. When you connect with others facing similar challenges, you can openly discuss your victories and setbacks without fear of judgment. Think about forming a group where members share their journeys toward authenticity. In these spaces, you can tell your stories, encourage one another, and celebrate every milestone, no matter how small.

As you navigate societal pressures, remember that it's okay to step back and evaluate your surroundings. Sometimes, the best way to stay true to yourself is to distance yourself from influences that undermine your authenticity. This might mean cutting back on certain social media platforms that hurt your self-esteem or having candid conversations with friends or family about how their expectations affect you.

Your well-being should always come first. Be unapologetic in your chase for happiness, and do what feels right for you. Acknowledge that while societal pressures may always be present, your commitment to authenticity is a powerful force that can help you rise above them.

As you journey toward honoring your personal choices, embrace the power of storytelling. Sharing your experiences—both the struggles and the triumphs—can help you connect with others and inspire them. Consider journaling your thoughts, creating a blog, or even starting a podcast to discuss your path toward authenticity. Your voice can resonate with those who might be grappling with similar issues, reminding them that they're not alone.

As you carve your path, don't forget to celebrate your uniqueness. Each step toward authenticity is a victory, no matter how small. Embrace the quirks that make you who you are, and take pride in the decisions you make. Your journey is about more than just overcoming societal pressures; it's about thriving in your true self.

So, as you move forward, remember that the world needs more people who are brave enough to be themselves. You have the strength to rise above the noise and assert the choices that align with your true self. Every time you choose authenticity over conformity, you plant seeds of inspiration in those around you. By staying true to your values, you not only reclaim your individuality but also help create a more vibrant and accepting society.

In this journey of self-discovery, remember you're not alone. Others are walking the same path, dealing with pressures that try to shape their lives. Together, you can foster a community of authenticity, resilience, and empowerment. As you move forward, trust in your ability to navigate societal pressures while remaining the beautiful, unique person you are. Embrace the challenges, celebrate your victories, and let your light shine brightly, inspiring others to do the same.

Faye Chandler

Chapter 7: The Digital Influence: Choices in a Tech-Driven World

The Role of Algorithms: Subtle Manipulations

In the complex world of our digital lives, algorithms act like hidden puppeteers, guiding the choices we make every day. These mathematical formulas and coded instructions aren't just abstract ideas from the realm of computer science; they weave their way into our routines, influencing everything from the movies we watch on Netflix to the products we shop for on Amazon, and even the news articles we read. While we often appreciate the convenience these technologies provide, it's time to take a closer look at the subtle ways they affect our choices.

Think back to the last time you browsed through your Netflix homepage. You probably saw a personalized selection of films and shows, all designed to match your tastes. The trailers play, colorful images flash, and before you know it, you're hooked on yet another series that feels just right for you. But how did those specific titles end up on your screen? The answer lies in the intricate algorithms that personalize your experience. These algorithms analyze your data—like your viewing history, the shows you rate highly, and your search queries—to predict what you might want to watch next. The result is a digital experience that feels so personal, like the platform knows you better than you know yourself.

However, this tailored selection can come at a price. By constantly presenting similar content, these algorithms can unintentionally create echo chambers, limiting our exposure to a wider variety of artistic expressions and ideas. Studies have shown that users often end up watching similar genres or themes, which can hinder their cultural growth. We might start with a simple wish to find something fun to watch, only to discover that our choices have become more and more similar over time. The algorithm softly reassures us that we're satisfied, while, without realizing it, it's quietly shaping our preferences.

A similar pattern emerges on shopping websites like Amazon. When you click on a product, the recommendations that follow aren't just random suggestions; they are carefully crafted predictions aimed at keeping you engaged and boosting sales. This algorithm-driven approach, backed by heaps of user data, creates a shopping experience that feels almost magical. You might begin with a straightforward search for a book, but soon you find yourself being nudged toward related items you never even thought about. "Customers who bought this item also bought..." becomes a tempting call, leading you down a path of impulsive decisions and unexpected purchases.

While this can lead to fun discoveries, it can also reinforce shopping habits that don't truly reflect our needs or values. The ease of having options presented to us can hide the fact that we're usually selecting from a limited range, missing out on alternatives that could bring us more satisfaction or meaning. The illusion of choice becomes clear when we realize that the algorithm, by design, has guided us toward specific outcomes that align with its goals—mainly, keeping us engaged and encouraging us to spend more.

The subtlety of these influences is perhaps most noticeable on social media platforms like Facebook and Instagram. Here, algorithms not only tailor the content we see but also shape the personas we create online. The endless scroll of customized posts crafts a reality that feels personal and relevant, yet it's often a twisted reflection of our real lives. Every like, comment, and share feeds into a complicated algorithm that learns our preferences, ultimately molding our online interactions in ways we might not fully understand.

Take a moment to think about social validation. Social media thrives on the excitement of likes and shares, and algorithms reward content that gathers attention. Users get a rush with every notification, creating a cycle that pushes them to engage more often and share more selectively. This behavior can be a double-edged sword; while we might feel a sense of belonging and connection, we're also caught in a web of curated experiences that don't always show our true selves.

The effects of these algorithms reach beyond our online lives and spill into our real-world decision-making. The way we interact with businesses, news sources, and even friends can be influenced by the tailored experiences we have online. When social media platforms prioritize certain voices and ideas, they unconsciously shape how we see the world. This becomes especially concerning when it comes to misinformation, as algorithms may highlight sensational content over accurate reporting simply because it attracts more clicks and engagement.

Real-life examples further highlight this issue. Consider a young adult trying to explore political opinions on social media. At first, they might follow a variety of voices; however, as the algorithms adapt to their preferences, they may end up trapped in a bubble where only certain viewpoints are highlighted. This narrowing of perspectives doesn't just limit their understanding of the world; it can also skew their decision-making. The outcome is a society that feels more divided and polarized, a trend with serious implications for us all.

As we navigate this digital terrain, it's crucial to be aware of how algorithms shape our choices. Understanding how these systems operate allows us to take back some control over our decisions. It's not about turning away from technology altogether; it's about building a more thoughtful relationship with the digital tools we use.

We can begin by actively seeking out diverse content and exploring options that differ from our usual preferences. If the algorithm only offers what we've already liked or bought, we should make a conscious effort to step outside those boundaries. Dedicating time to discover unfamiliar genres, engage with contrasting viewpoints, or consider alternative products can widen our perspectives and enrich our experiences.

Moreover, we can push for greater transparency from technology companies. By asking these platforms to explain how their algorithms work, we can create a more informed user community that understands the effects of their digital choices. When users grasp the underlying mechanics, they can make more intentional decisions—whether that means curating their social media feeds, diversifying their entertainment, or making thoughtful purchases.

The digital age brings incredible opportunities and significant challenges. As algorithms continue to develop, they will play an increasingly important role in shaping our preferences and decisions. However, by nurturing critical thinking and staying aware of the subtle influences at play, we can navigate this landscape with more insight and intention.

Ultimately, it's about reclaiming our power in a world increasingly guided by algorithmic influence. Our preferences and choices should resonate with who we really are, not just be byproducts of invisible systems that manipulate our desires. As we cultivate this awareness, we can begin to untangle our identities from the algorithms that seek to shape them, creating lives that reflect our true dreams and values in a tech-driven world.

Technology and Self-Image: Implications for Personal Choices

The rise of social media has changed how we show ourselves and connect with others. Platforms like Instagram, Facebook, and TikTok have turned into modern-day stages where people share their lives, which can inspire both empowerment and deep insecurity. The polished photos and carefully crafted captions we see every day can distort our view of reality, creating a world where what's ideal isn't just shown—it's expected. While scrolling through endless feeds, we can't help but wonder: how does this constant exposure to perfectly curated lives affect our self-image and influence our personal decisions?

Social comparisons have become a big part of our social media experience. In the past, we might have only compared ourselves to a small circle of friends and family. Now, the digital world opens that circle to an infinite number of polished lives. It's easy to forget that the images we see are often just snapshots of selected moments, designed to tell a certain story. Take Mia, for example. At just twenty-two, she feels the pressure to showcase a perfect life on her Instagram feed, filled with beautiful landscapes, flawless selfies, and enviable adventures. She spends hours planning her outings just to capture that perfect shot for social media, editing her photos until they look immaculate. But underneath it all, Mia struggles with feelings of inadequacy as she compares herself to the seemingly perfect lives of those around her.

When Mia scrolls through her feed, she starts to question her own worth, her choices, and her achievements. The pressure builds as she sees friends and influencers living lives that appear picture-perfect. This constant comparison can lead to a harmful cycle of dissatisfaction. When we stack ourselves up against others—especially when all we see are the highlights—it's easy to overlook our own accomplishments and unique traits. Instead, we end up focusing on what we perceive as our shortcomings, feeling as though we can never measure up to an impossible standard. This struggle with comparison isn't just Mia's alone; it's something many people face in today's digital age, leading to a shared sense of self-doubt.

The emotional impact of these comparisons goes beyond temporary insecurity. Research suggests that those who frequently engage in social comparison are more likely to experience anxiety and depression. Mia, for instance, began to see how this cycle affected her mental health. The need to present herself in a way that fit social media expectations started to take over her genuine interests and passions. As her self-worth became tied to online approval, she made choices that didn't truly reflect who she was, simply to chase likes and comments.

The term "fear of missing out," or FOMO, captures a significant issue in the social media age. FOMO is rooted in the belief that everyone else is living a more exciting life filled with experiences that you're missing out on. Constant notifications about parties, gatherings, and adventures can make one feel like their own life is lacking. Mia found herself attending events she didn't even care about, just to avoid missing out on what she thought was fun and fulfilling for others. This pressure to be always "on" can lead to choices that focus more on fitting in with a social narrative than on personal satisfaction.

The search for external validation is another important factor in understanding how technology affects our self-image. The need for approval through likes, comments, and shares can warp our sense of worth. For Mia, that rush she felt with each notification turned into a double-edged sword. What initially boosted her self-esteem soon became a dependency that left her feeling exhausted and anxious. The thrill of online engagement was like a rollercoaster; it gave her moments of joy but also left her feeling low when the excitement faded.

Studies show that the more someone leans on social media for validation, the more they may feel unhappy with their self-image. This connection is especially strong among younger users who are still figuring out who they are. For Mia, the moment her self-worth became tied to her online presence marked a turning point. She began to believe her value was directly linked to her online persona, leading her to make choices that didn't truly represent who she was.

As we think about this phenomenon, it's important to consider practical steps we can take for a healthier relationship with social media. Being intentional about our digital interactions can change how we see ourselves and the decisions we make. One effective strategy is to curate our social media feeds to follow individuals and messages that promote self-acceptance and authenticity, rather than those that push unrealistic standards. By choosing the content we consume, we can create a digital space that supports our well-being instead of undermining it.

Additionally, practicing self-compassion is crucial to counter the negative effects of comparison. Mia learned to remind herself that everyone has their struggles, often hidden behind a mask of perfection. Realizing this became a key part of her journey to reclaiming her self-image. Instead of giving in to the pressure to compare, she began to celebrate her own unique experiences and growth. Understanding that her worth isn't tied to the carefully curated images others share online was a powerful step toward self-acceptance.

Recognizing the temporary nature of online validation can also change our viewpoint. While likes and comments might seem important, their fleeting nature highlights the value of building deeper relationships and pursuing the activities that genuinely bring us joy. Mia gradually shifted her focus from seeking digital approval to embracing the richness of real-life connections. By prioritizing authentic relationships and experiences that resonated with her values, she started to regain her sense of self beyond the limits of social media.

The link between technology and self-image is certainly complex, woven into our daily lives in meaningful ways. It affects our choices, our identity, and our overall happiness. As we navigate this expansive digital world, it's vital to be aware of the influences at play and make deliberate choices that honor who we are as individuals. By nurturing a more mindful relationship with social media, we can start breaking down the unhealthy patterns that affect our digital lives, opening the door to a more authentic existence that goes beyond the lens of curated perfection.

Ultimately, the goal isn't to cut out technology but to engage with it in a way that uplifts rather than diminishes our self-worth. As we explore how our digital interactions impact us, let's embrace the idea that our choices don't have to be dictated by the curated stories we see online. Instead, we can choose to cultivate a sense of self that is grounded in authenticity, resilience, and genuine connection. The journey to reclaiming our self-image in a tech-driven world might have its challenges, but it also holds the potential for profound transformation—a renewal of self that isn't overshadowed by the pressures of digital comparison.

Personalization in Marketing: Effects on Consumer Habits

In the constantly changing world of marketing, the rise of personalization has fundamentally changed how businesses connect with their customers. The days of generic ads that attempt to appeal to everyone are long gone. Nowadays, companies gather and analyze data in ways that allow them to tailor their advertisements with incredible precision, targeting us as individuals in ways we never imagined. The magic of algorithms has brought us to a point where our online behavior not only influences the products presented to us but can also shape our everyday choices.

Picture this: you're scrolling through your social media feed, and suddenly, you spot an ad for those shoes you admired a few weeks back but didn't buy. How did that ad find its way to you? The answer lies in the clever techniques that brands use to gather details about our online habits. Every click, every scroll, and even the time we spend hovering over an item on a webpage is carefully tracked. This information helps marketers build a profile that reveals not just what we desire but what they believe we need. It's both fascinating and a bit unsettling; we become active players in a system designed to persuade us to spend more.

Consider those targeted ads that seem to pop up out of nowhere. While it might feel like coincidence, these ads are actually the result of complex algorithms that are built to learn our preferences and habits. For example, a user who frequently interacts with fitness-related posts is likely to see ads for gym memberships, workout gear, or health supplements. The algorithm has figured out what interests this user and is now eager to guide them toward making a purchase. But what happens when this personalization edges into manipulation?

The ethical questions surrounding personalized marketing raise important issues about the thin line between customization and pressure. Are we genuinely being catered to, or are we subtly nudged to follow a brand's agenda? Take the "scarcity effect," for example—a psychological trick where consumers value items more when they think they are limited or hard to find. Marketers exploit this behavior by creating a sense of urgency—think limited-time offers or alerts about low stock—leading consumers to make quick choices driven by the fear of missing out. When faced with the possibility of losing something they want, many people act impulsively, snatching up products without really considering if they genuinely need them.

Additionally, marketers use the "decoy effect," a pricing strategy that influences our choices by introducing a third option that makes the other two look more appealing. Imagine a subscription service offering three plans: a basic plan at $10 per month, a premium plan at $20, and a third plan with similar features to the premium plan but priced at $30. The decoy plan may lead consumers to choose the premium option, thinking it's the best deal, all while skipping over the basic plan. This subtle nudging can shape our decisions without us even realizing it.

While personalization can make shopping more enjoyable, it's crucial for consumers to stay alert. Being aware of these tactics can help us make informed choices instead of being swept away by clever marketing. The aim isn't to banish all advertising from our lives—after all, notifications about sales on our favorite brands can be genuinely helpful—but to cultivate a more thoughtful approach to shopping.

To navigate this complex marketing world, one simple step is to adopt a more conscious consumer mindset. Take a moment to think about the ads you often see and whether they truly match your values and needs. Are you genuinely interested in that product, or are you just reacting to a well-crafted sales pitch? By actively considering your buying choices, you take back control over your consumer habits.

Another useful strategy is to widen your sources of information. The more viewpoints you encounter, the better you can recognize when you're being directed toward a specific choice. For instance, if you're looking for a new laptop, it's easy to get distracted by ads for the latest models from big tech companies. Instead, seek out user reviews, independent blog posts, and comparison articles that offer in-depth insights into what's available. This broader perspective helps you make decisions based on what you really want rather than what marketers are promoting.

Mindfulness practices can also help you resist manipulative marketing tactics. By being aware of your emotional responses, you can tell the difference between what you truly want and what's being pushed onto you. For example, if you feel a rush of excitement when you see an ad for a new gadget, take a second to pause. Ask yourself why you're drawn to this item. Is it a real need, or just the result of clever advertising? This simple habit of reflection can provide a buffer against impulsive buys.

Talking with friends or family about marketing strategies can also create a sense of community awareness. Sharing stories about marketing influences can reveal patterns that might go unnoticed on our own. By voicing our experiences, we encourage a culture of thoughtful consumerism, empowering ourselves and others to make smarter choices.

In the end, as personalized marketing continues to shape our shopping experiences, it's important for consumers to understand the dynamics at play. Knowing how the ads that surround us work can help shield us from manipulative tactics. With mindfulness, critical thinking, and supportive conversations, we can become savvy shoppers who move through the marketplace with purpose, making choices that truly reflect who we are.

Chapter 8: The Role of Habits in Decision-Making

The Science of Habit Formation: Empowering Choices

Habits shape our everyday lives, often guiding our actions and decisions without us even realizing it. Think about your morning routine: you wake up and instinctively grab your phone, scrolling through social media before you've even had a chance to brush your teeth. This ritual is so ingrained that it hardly crosses your mind, yet it sets the mood for your entire day. This simple example shows just how much our habits influence not only what we do but also how we feel about ourselves.

At their core, habits are behaviors that become automatic because we repeat them over and over. They follow a three-part cycle: cue, routine, and reward. This model, known as the habit loop, helps us understand how our habits form. The cue is what triggers us to start a behavior; the routine is the behavior itself; and the reward is the positive feeling we get afterward that reinforces the habit. With time, this loop becomes hardwired in our brains, making the behavior feel almost instinctive and often hard to resist.

Let's break this down a bit more. Cues can be anything from a specific time of day to how we're feeling or even things in our environment. For example, you might notice that whenever you sit down at your desk, the sight of a candy jar makes you reach for a sweet treat. The routine is snacking, and it's followed by the immediate reward: the enjoyable taste of candy and that little sugar rush that feels like a boost. This simple yet powerful loop shows how our brains prefer familiar paths over trying something new.

Research into psychology digs into the science behind habits. When we repeat actions, neurons in our brains connect, creating links that get stronger over time. This makes it easier for us to do these actions without even thinking about them. Think about that morning routine with your phone: each time you swipe the screen, the connections between those neurons strengthen, until it feels completely natural.

Now, let's look at a real-life example that shows how understanding habits can change our lives. Meet Sarah, a hardworking marketing professional who realized she was stuck in a cycle of mindless snacking at work. Every day, around mid-morning, she would unconsciously reach for a bag of chips, only to feel unsatisfied and regretful an hour later. Recognizing this pattern was her first big step. The cue? Sitting at her desk after her morning coffee. The routine? Snacking without thinking. And the reward? A quick hit of taste and satisfaction, quickly followed by guilt.

With this new awareness, Sarah decided to make a change. She identified her cue and chose to switch up her routine. Instead of reaching for the chips, she promised herself a five-minute walk around the office building whenever she felt the urge to snack. This small change introduced a new routine that not only got her moving but also refreshed her mind. The new reward, while different, became the boost of energy and focus she felt when she returned to her desk.

Sarah's experience teaches us an important lesson: habits aren't set in stone; they can change. The secret is to identify the cues that spark our behaviors and consciously replace the routines that aren't helping us anymore.

This brings us to the two-sided nature of habits. They can be empowering, but they can also create obstacles that hold us back. Insights from behavioral economics show how our habits can lead us down the wrong path. For instance, if you often procrastinate, it might be because you've developed a habit of scrolling through social media instead of tackling your work. The cue could be the stress of an approaching deadline, the routine is putting things off, and the reward is that brief escape from pressure. Understanding this cycle can help us find ways to change.

By understanding our habits, we can align our actions with what we truly want. When we uncover the automatic behaviors that drive us, we gain the ability to break free from doubt and negativity. By reshaping our habits intentionally, we empower ourselves to make choices that reflect our values and long-term goals.

Research by psychologist Wendy Wood, who has studied habits in depth, reveals that nearly 45% of our daily actions are driven by habit. This surprising statistic shows just how much habits control our lives, often without us even being aware. Knowing this can feel freeing because it means we can use habits to our advantage.

Let's also explore the idea of habit stacking, a handy technique for building new positive behaviors. The idea is straightforward: you build a new habit on top of an existing one. For example, if you already brew coffee every morning, you could stack a new habit of practicing gratitude by taking a moment to write down three things you're thankful for while your coffee brews. This approach taps into your current routine, making it more likely that the new behavior will stick.

Habit stacking is a practical way to encourage consistency and can lead to a more fulfilling life. By building on what you already do, you can make it easier to create healthier habits. It allows you to take advantage of your brain's existing pathways, requiring less conscious effort while still enabling you to make significant changes.

As we think about habits, it becomes clear that recognizing their influence in our lives is vital. By shaping our habits with care, we can change how we make decisions and, ultimately, how we live. The ability to spot cues, transform routines, and set new rewards is a powerful skill that gives us control over our choices.

Learning about how habits form not only helps us understand our own behaviors but also gives us the tools to make meaningful changes in our lives. This journey isn't just about breaking bad habits or starting new ones; it's about grasping the deeper mechanics that influence our choices. By being aware of our habits, we embark on a path of self-discovery and purpose.

It's through this perspective that we can truly take charge of our decisions. When we look at our habits with clarity and intention, we unlock the potential for real change. Just like Sarah learned, and many others have found, our habits can be used to create lives filled with purpose, authenticity, and fulfillment.

Breaking and Building Habits: Practical Techniques

Habits can be like familiar trails through a forest—they can lead us toward growth and happiness or trap us in cycles where we feel stuck. Whether it's that comforting first cup of coffee in the morning, scrolling through social media, or binge-watching Netflix at night, our daily routines are often guided by habits we don't even notice. But here's the good news: while habits can be powerful, they aren't permanent. With the right strategies, we can break free from negative patterns and carve out new paths for positive change.

One helpful strategy is the 21/90 rule. This straightforward guideline suggests it takes about 21 days to form a new habit and 90 days to make it a part of your life. Think of it as a guiding light for anyone eager to create change. The initial 21 days can be tough as you work to set a new routine, navigating through temptations and distractions. But those next 90 days are where the real transformation happens, solidifying that new habit and weaving it into the core of your daily life.

Picture changing a tough habit as a journey. The first 21 days can feel like the hardest part of a climb: the air feels thin, the path is steep, and each step seems like a huge effort. But as you push through, gaining momentum and strength, you'll find your rhythm. The next six weeks are where the magic starts. These days build on your hard work, turning the struggle into a natural part of your life. This is a process of growth, where the new habit feels like second nature, and the discomfort of change shifts into the comfort of routine.

Let's take a look at Alex's story. He's a graphic designer who had a knack for procrastination. He often found himself lost in design blogs, delaying projects until the last moment. Ready for a change, Alex decided to follow the 21/90 rule. He made a goal to dedicate at least 30 minutes every morning to work on his projects without distractions. The first three weeks were a real challenge. He fought the urge to check his phone or get sidetracked by online distractions. But he didn't give up. By the end of those 21 days, something shifted. His work sessions became easier, even enjoyable. Fast forward to 90 days later, and his focused work time became an essential part of his daily routine, leading to better work and a more balanced life.

What's great about the 21/90 rule is how simple and rewarding it is. It breaks down the daunting task of changing habits into manageable steps, where each day feels like a small win that builds on the last. It encourages patience—because real change takes time, and recognizing the effort you put in is a key part of the journey.

Of course, challenges are bound to pop up as you work on changing habits. That's where the idea of implementation intentions comes in. This technique helps you pre-plan your responses to obstacles, creating a mental game plan for success. It involves making "if-then" statements that guide your actions when old habits try to creep back in.

For example, if you're working on exercising regularly, a common hurdle might be the temptation to skip a workout after a long day. Using implementation intentions, you could say, "If it's 6:00 PM and I feel tired, then I will change into my workout clothes and do at least 10 minutes of exercise." This way, you're ready to tackle challenges before they arise, turning potential setbacks into chances to succeed.

Maria's story is a great example of this technique. She's a busy mom with two kids who struggled to keep up with her fitness routine. Juggling family demands made it hard for her to stick to regular workouts. After learning about implementation intentions, Maria came up with her own plans. She decided that if she felt too tired to go for a run after dinner, she would at least do a quick 10-minute yoga session in her living room. This small commitment kept her connected to her goal without overwhelming her. Over time, those 10 minutes turned into longer sessions, making exercise a valued part of her daily life.

Another key piece of building habits is setting SMART goals—those that are Specific, Measurable, Achievable, Relevant, and Time-bound. This approach helps you clarify your goals and track your progress in a meaningful way. Instead of saying, "I want to read more," a SMART goal would be, "I will read one book per month for the next six months." This kind of goal provides clarity and sets you up for accountability.

Kevin's journey highlights the power of SMART goals. He's an aspiring writer who often felt lost in his creative dreams. He wanted to finish a novel but was overwhelmed by his own ambitions and lack of a plan. After attending a workshop on goal-setting, Kevin decided to break down his big goal into SMART goals. He committed to writing 500 words each day, five days a week, for three months. This clear, measurable, and time-bound goal turned his writing from an abstract dream into a reality. Each day brought him closer to his dream, and by the end of three months, he had completed a full draft of his novel.

These personal stories remind us that using techniques like the 21/90 rule, implementation intentions, and SMART goals can lead to impressive changes. The common theme here is that change isn't just about willpower; it's about using smart strategies that help us take charge of our habits and goals. The real power of these techniques lies in how they provide a clear path for anyone looking to improve their lives.

As you go through your own journey of changing habits, take some time to reflect. Think about the habits you want to change and those you want to develop. Ask yourself questions like: What habits are holding me back? What new habits do I want to build? What triggers my current routines? Reflecting on these questions can help you understand your motivations and goals better.

Consider jotting down your thoughts. Writing things down can make your intentions feel more real and strengthen your commitment to change. After identifying the habits you want to adjust, use the techniques we've talked about. Challenge yourself for 21 days, create implementation intentions, and set SMART goals. Every step you take is a testament to your determination and strength.

Ultimately, the journey of breaking and building habits is about making progress, not achieving perfection. It's about understanding that slips might happen, but what matters most is that you keep moving forward. The grace to stumble and the strength to get back up define the process of personal growth. Embrace your journey, celebrate your wins, and remember that every small change adds to the bigger story of your life.

So, whether you're taking on the challenge of a new habit or trying to shake off an old one, remember: you're not alone. Many have walked this path before you, and with the right strategies, you can create a life that truly reflects your values and dreams.

Habit Stacking: Enhancing Success through Combination

Imagine waking up each day, not overwhelmed by a chaotic rush of thoughts but instead feeling a sense of calm as you move smoothly from one productive habit to the next. Habit stacking can help you achieve this peaceful routine, turning everyday tasks into purposeful actions that drive you toward your goals. By cleverly pairing a new habit with an existing one, you create a strong connection that makes positive changes feel easy and natural.

Let's take a closer look at how habit stacking works. The idea is simple yet incredibly effective. You find a routine that's already part of your life—something you do without even thinking—and add a new behavior you want to develop right on top of it. This approach not only lessens the mental effort required to start a new habit but also builds on the momentum of your established routines. It's like adding a delicious topping to your favorite ice cream; the base is already enjoyable, but the extra flavor makes it even better.

To start using habit stacking, first identify your current habits. What do you do every day without fail? Maybe it's that morning coffee ritual, or perhaps you always check your emails right after lunch. With these daily anchors in mind, think about new habits you'd like to add. The combinations are endless, and the results can be truly life-changing.

Take your morning coffee routine, for instance. Instead of simply savoring that cherished cup of caffeine by yourself, why not pair it with a gratitude practice? Each morning, as you brew your coffee, take a moment to write down three things you're thankful for in a journal. This small addition can shift your mindset, filling your day with positivity from the very start. Picture how that uplifting feeling could follow you during your morning commute, into meetings, and beyond. By connecting gratitude to something you already do, you create an easy transition that sets a positive tone for the day.

Many successful people have used habit stacking to boost their productivity and well-being. Take productivity experts, for example, who often highlight the power of morning routines. Tim Ferriss, well-known for his book "The 4-Hour Workweek," encourages starting your day with mindful practices. He suggests pairing a few minutes of meditation with your morning shower. While washing away the sleepiness of the night, you can clear your mind and focus on your intentions for the day ahead. This simple combination not only makes the most of your time but also brings a sense of mental clarity that can help you tackle your work with focus.

Wellness coaches also stress the importance of linking healthy eating habits with your existing routines. For instance, if you usually watch TV in the evening, you might combine that with a goal of preparing a healthy snack. Instead of reaching for chips or sweets, you could whip up a bowl of sliced fruits or veggies. The act of cutting and arranging your snack can become a calming ritual as you enjoy your favorite show. Before long, this new behavior could feel just as natural as turning on the TV.

The perks of habit stacking go beyond just making new habits easier to adopt; they also create a sense of achievement that boosts your motivation. When you succeed in one area, it often spills over into other aspects of your life, creating a wave of positivity. This is especially true when the new habit delivers immediate rewards, tapping into your brain's reward system. That little thrill of completing a successful stack can motivate you to take on even bigger challenges.

Now, let's talk about consistency. With habit stacking, you're tapping into the power of repetition. The more you practice stacking, the easier it becomes to fold new behaviors into your life. Over time, the initial effort fades, allowing you to focus on enjoying the benefits. Just like Alex, the graphic designer, who changed his mornings by dedicating thirty minutes to focused work, you might find that your stacked habits become beloved parts of your daily routine.

If you're feeling hesitant about starting this journey, reflecting on your habits can be a game changer. It might seem intimidating to think about where to begin, but take a moment to write down your daily routines. Which ones feel automatic? Which ones do you enjoy? Are there any that you'd like to enhance or change? This exercise can reveal potential areas for stacking, guiding you toward effective combinations that fit your lifestyle.

Imagine reviewing your evening routine and realizing you'd like to include reading in your life. Instead of trying to carve out an entirely new hour for reading, you could attach this new habit to your nighttime wind-down routine. As you settle into bed, you might decide to read a few pages of a book after brushing your teeth. This gentle addition can help cultivate a love for reading without the pressure of altering your entire bedtime ritual.

The beauty of habit stacking is that it empowers you to take control of your life in small, manageable steps. It's not about overhauling everything at once; it's about celebrating the small victories that help you reach your bigger goals. This method can be especially helpful for those who feel overwhelmed by trying to make big changes. Rather than feeling like you're trying to climb a mountain, habit stacking allows you to take one small step at a time, gradually building your strengths and skills.

As you start stacking your habits, it's important to stay flexible. Life can be unpredictable, and what works for you today might not be effective tomorrow. It's perfectly fine to make adjustments, swap one habit for another, or even let go of a stack that no longer serves you. The key is to stay in tune with your needs and motivations, allowing your habit stacks to grow and change just like you do.

Stories of people who have successfully used habit stacking can inspire you to start your own journey. For example, consider Lisa, a nurse who struggled to balance her demanding job with her desire for fitness. Each morning, she rushed out the door, often skipping breakfast. Realizing this challenge, Lisa decided to stack her breakfast routine with her coffee habit. While brewing her morning cup, she began making a smoothie filled with nutrients. Blending her smoothie while waiting for her coffee transformed her mornings, giving her energy and nourishment as she headed to work. Over time, this new stack became a vital part of her daily routine, fueling her both physically and mentally.

At this point, you might be inspired to think of habit stacks for your own life. Reflect on the habits you already have and creatively consider what new behaviors you want to introduce. What existing routines could serve as a springboard for your new aspirations? Maybe you could stack a moment of mindfulness or meditation onto your daily commute, or you might want to take a few minutes to stretch after lunch. Let your imagination roam as you explore these possibilities.

Keep in mind that forming new habits through stacking is not a race. It requires patience and kindness toward yourself. Enjoy the journey, celebrate the small wins, and remember that bumps in the road are a normal part of the process. You might find that some stacks thrive while others need tweaking or even scrapping altogether. This is all part of learning and growing.

As you begin your habit stacking journey, consider keeping a journal to track your progress and reflect on your experiences. Writing down your thoughts can strengthen your commitment to change and provide valuable insights as you navigate your habits. You might record how stacking different habits feels, the challenges you face, and how you can continue to develop. This reflective practice can deepen your understanding and enhance your ability to make lasting changes.

In the end, habit stacking is about using your existing routines to build new behaviors that match your values and aspirations. It's about realizing that personal growth doesn't have to be difficult; instead, it can be a series of small, thoughtful steps that lead to significant changes over time. With each stack you create, you're not just changing your routine; you're reshaping how you approach life.

As you think about your current habits and potential stacks, remember that you have the power to transform your daily experiences. By thoughtfully combining habits, you can make choices that align with your goals and dreams. So take a moment to reflect on your habits, embrace the practice of stacking, and get ready to enjoy the transformation that comes from living with intention. With each new stack, you'll find yourself closer to the life you envision—a life filled with purpose, fulfillment, and the agency to shape your choices.

Chapter 9: Harnessing the Power of Reflection

Analyzing Past Decisions: Motivation and Outcomes

Life is a collection of choices, some small and some life-changing, but all of them come together to shape who we are. Every decision we make is driven by a mix of motivations, desires, and situations that, when we look closely, can reveal deep insights into our values and beliefs. Reflecting on our choices becomes a valuable tool that helps us understand the paths we've taken and the reasons behind them.

Think back to a time when you made a big decision. Maybe you took a new job, moved to a different city, or ended a long-term relationship. During moments like these, we often find ourselves caught in a whirlwind of emotions and thoughts. Some days we feel sure about our choices; other days, we might feel lost. The reasons we make these choices can vary widely, influenced by our past experiences, what society expects, and what we truly want.

In our daily lives, we are often guided by both our conscious thoughts and our gut feelings. Take, for example, the story of Sarah, a young woman who was given a chance to move up in her career. She accepted a new job that seemed perfect to her: better pay, more responsibilities, and the opportunity to work with respected colleagues. However, a few months in, Sarah felt unfulfilled and started to doubt her decision. What led her to take this leap? Was it the appeal of status, pressure from friends, or a genuine love for her work?

Through reflecting on her choices, Sarah uncovered motivations she hadn't seen before. She came to realize that while she was excited about moving forward in her career, her choice was tied to a need for validation from others. The fear of being viewed as stagnant had blurred her judgment, leading her to value others' approval over her own interests. This insight was more than just thinking back on her past; it was a turning point that allowed Sarah to realign her career with what she truly wanted.

Understanding how our minds work when making decisions is key to becoming more self-aware. For example, cognitive biases can greatly affect how we view our choices and what we expect from them. The confirmation bias is one such bias that makes us look for information that backs up our beliefs while ignoring what doesn't fit. This can distort how we see our decisions, making it hard to understand why we chose what we did. Recognizing these biases during our self-reflection can help us gain clarity and create a more accurate story of our past.

When we take the time to reflect, it can be helpful to use structured methods that guide us through the process. Journaling is one of the best ways to capture our thoughts and feelings about specific decisions. By writing down the context of a choice, the emotions we felt at the time, and what happened afterward, we create a record we can revisit. This practice sharpens our focus and allows us to see patterns in our decision-making over time.

Picture yourself sitting down with a notebook, pen ready, and letting your thoughts spill out. Think about the important decisions you've made in the past year. What drove you to make those choices? What were the results, and how did they measure up against your expectations? This reflective practice invites you to dive deeper into the relationship between your motivations and results, revealing insights that might otherwise stay hidden.

For Sarah, journaling became a vital tool on her journey toward understanding herself better. Each entry peeled back another layer of her motivations, uncovering the fears and desires that shaped her choices. As she explored her feelings about her job, she recognized that it was crucial to align her career with her true self, rather than simply chasing external validation. This process of self-analysis not only gave her a better understanding of her past decisions but also guided her future choices.

Another valuable technique to enhance reflection is meditation. Taking just a few quiet moments each day to sit in stillness can provide the mental space we need for contemplation. During these sessions, we can focus on specific decisions, letting our thoughts and feelings come up without judgment. This mindfulness practice helps us become more aware, allowing us to observe our thoughts as they arise instead of getting caught up in them. With this greater awareness, we can start to see the motivations behind our decisions more clearly.

To illustrate how meditation can aid decision-making, let's look at Mark, a middle-aged professional facing a career change. He was constantly stressed about making the "right" choice, worried that any wrong turn could derail his future. Seeking relief, Mark began to meditate each morning, taking a few minutes to reflect on his options. As he sat quietly, he learned to drown out the external noise and listen to his own instincts. This practice helped him identify his core values and aspirations, ultimately leading him to a decision that felt genuine and fulfilling.

The relationship between motivation and outcomes is often influenced by the situation in which decisions are made. Life circumstances, social pressures, and even the passage of time can change how we view our options and the motivations behind them. For example, a choice made in a moment of desperation might look very different later when the emotions have settled and a clearer perspective emerges.

Reflecting on the context of our decisions can be particularly enlightening during pivotal moments in our lives. Consider Jamie, who had long dreamed of starting her own business. After years in a stable job, she finally took the leap, fueled by passion and a desire for independence. At first, everything seemed to go well, but as challenges mounted, Jamie started to question her choice. Was her motivation based on true passion, or was it a reaction to the boredom of her corporate job? This realization pushed Jamie to reflect on what had influenced her decision. She discovered that her choice was as much about escaping an unsatisfactory situation as it was about following her dreams.

Through reflection, Jamie gained insight into her motivations and the circumstances that pushed her to start her own business. By understanding the complexities of her decision-making process, she could adjust her goals and strategies, creating a path that more closely aligned with her true self. This level of awareness is what reflection can offer—a clear mirror showing not just our choices but the intricate web of motivations and contexts that shape them.

While it can be tempting to see our past decisions as strict markers of success or failure, it's crucial to understand that they are stepping stones on our journey. Each choice gives us a chance to learn, grow, and deepen our understanding of ourselves. Reflection helps us turn what we view as mistakes into valuable lessons, prompting us to look inward and uncover the reasons behind our actions.

By practicing reflection, we can sharpen our awareness of our motivations and the outcomes of our decisions. This self-discovery empowers us to make choices that align with our core values and aspirations. As we become more in tune with our internal compass, we gain the ability to navigate life's complexities with greater clarity, confidence, and authenticity.

There is real power in looking back at our choices—not with criticism but with curiosity and kindness. By analyzing our past decisions, we can uncover the motivations that guided us and the lessons that flowed from the outcomes. This reflective process enriches our understanding and equips us to make choices that are not only informed but also resonate with our true selves. As we embrace this path of self-discovery, we open the door to a more authentic and fulfilling life, one decision at a time.

Mindfulness and Awareness: Improving Decision Quality

In a world that often feels chaotic and overwhelming, where distractions are everywhere and life seems to speed up with each passing day, the idea of mindfulness arrives like a refreshing breeze, encouraging us to pause, take a breath, and truly connect with the moment we're in. At its heart, mindfulness is about being present and aware of our thoughts, feelings, and surroundings without judging them. It may sound simple, but its impact on decision-making can be significant, helping us make better choices through increased awareness.

Picture yourself trying to navigate a bustling city with a map, only to find every street corner filled with vibrant distractions pulling your attention away from where you want to go. This is similar to the mind caught in the whirlwind of daily life—rushed, anxious, and overwhelmed by all that's going on. Practicing mindfulness helps us refocus our attention, allowing us to see our path more clearly and cutting through the noise that can cloud our judgment.

Mindfulness's role in decision-making is crucial. Research shows that being mindful can reduce cognitive biases and improve clarity. By calming the mental chatter, we open up space for more thoughtful and deliberate choices. Our brains, that complex network of neurons, respond positively to mindfulness practices. Studies indicate that regular mindfulness practice can boost the functioning of the prefrontal cortex—the part of our brain responsible for higher-level thinking, including decision-making. As we grow in mindfulness, we become better at weighing our options, thinking about the possible outcomes, and making choices that truly reflect who we are.

But how does this shift happen in our brains? When we practice mindfulness, we activate specific areas that help with emotional control and flexible thinking. This activation leads to a clearer, more effective decision-making process. One study found that people who practiced mindfulness had less activity in the amygdala, the brain's emotional center, which often leads to impulsive reactions fueled by fear or anxiety. As we make mindfulness a habit, the noise of emotional reactivity quiets down, paving the way for a more balanced and rational approach to our decisions.

Cognitive biases, those sneaky distortions that shape our views and judgments, can easily steer us off course when making choices. A common example is confirmation bias, which leads us to seek out information that supports what we already believe while ignoring contradictory evidence. Mindfulness counters this by encouraging an open and curious mindset that allows us to consider different perspectives and evaluate information more fairly. By becoming aware of our cognitive biases through mindfulness, we empower ourselves to make decisions that are not only more informed but also more in line with our true intentions.

Of course, reaping the benefits of mindfulness isn't just an academic exercise; it requires practical application and consistent effort. Developing a mindful approach to decision-making is much like nurturing a garden; it takes time, care, and dedication. There's no quick fix for cultivating mindfulness; instead, it's a gradual journey that grows with our efforts. To help you bring mindfulness into your daily life, let's explore some practical exercises that can boost awareness and improve the quality of your decisions.

One of the simplest yet most powerful practices is conscious breathing. You can do this exercise anywhere and anytime—before a big meeting, during a break in a busy day, or even while thinking about a decision. Just find a comfortable position, close your eyes, and focus on your breath. Inhale deeply through your nose, allowing your belly to rise, and then exhale slowly through your mouth. As you breathe, pay attention to the sensations—notice the coolness of the air entering your nostrils, feel your lungs expanding, and notice the gentle release as you exhale.

When thoughts about the future or regrets about the past pop up in your mind, acknowledge them without judgment and gently bring your focus back to your breath. This simple yet powerful exercise grounds you in the present, helping you cultivate a sense of calm and clarity that can greatly influence your decision-making.

Grounding exercises provide another way to practice mindfulness. These techniques help keep us anchored in the moment, especially when we feel overwhelmed. One effective grounding exercise involves using your senses to reconnect with your environment. Take a moment to notice three things you can see, three things you can hear, and three things you can feel. This sensory awareness can help shift your focus from racing thoughts to the present moment, quieting the noise and enhancing your decision-making clarity.

Mindfulness doesn't require hours of our day. Even brief moments of focused awareness can bring significant benefits. Consider taking a mindful walk—one where you pay attention solely to the act of walking. Feel your feet on the ground, notice the rhythm of your breath, and listen to the sounds of nature around you. This practice can create mental space for reflection, allowing you to approach decisions with a more thoughtful mindset.

As we dive into mindful decision-making, it's clear that the benefits go beyond just making better choices. Mindfulness can change how we connect with ourselves and others, creating a ripple effect in our lives. When we approach decisions thoughtfully, we build greater self-awareness, helping us understand our motivations and desires more clearly. This self-awareness is a powerful tool, enabling us to identify what truly matters to us and navigate our choices with authenticity.

Consider the stories of people who have embraced mindfulness to improve their decision-making. Take Lisa, for instance, who found herself at a crossroads in her career. Although she had always loved teaching, societal pressures led her to pursue a corporate job instead. After a few years of feeling unfulfilled, Lisa discovered mindfulness practices that helped her uncover her true desires. Through meditation and reflection, she recognized that her heart longed to connect with others through education. Embracing mindfulness allowed her to return to teaching, leading her to a more fulfilling and purposeful life.

Then there's David, who faced a difficult personal choice about a relationship. Overwhelmed by emotions, he found it hard to think clearly. Through mindfulness practices, he learned to observe his feelings without judgment, giving himself a much-needed perspective. This newfound awareness helped him navigate the complexities of his relationship with a clear mind, resulting in a decision that honored both his heart and his values.

These stories demonstrate the transformative power of mindfulness in decision-making. The common thread is the deep self-awareness that mindfulness fosters. By enhancing their ability to observe their thoughts and emotions critically, both Lisa and David made decisions that were not just logical but also deeply connected to their true selves.

As we embrace mindfulness and its role in decision-making, we must remember that this journey is not a one-time event; it's an ongoing practice. Just like any skill, mindfulness needs to be nurtured and practiced consistently. It's easy to fall back into old habits of rushing or reacting without thinking, especially in a world that often encourages speed. However, by committing to small acts of mindfulness each day, we can gradually reshape our decision-making habits, allowing them to be more deliberate, balanced, and authentic.

Every mindful breath we take and every moment we dedicate to self-reflection paves the way for greater clarity and insight. Taking a moment to pause—whether it's to breathe, observe our surroundings, or check in with ourselves—can lead to profound revelations about our motivations and desires. It is often in these quiet moments that we discover the answers we've been searching for.

Furthermore, the connection between mindfulness and decision-making extends beyond our individual choices; it also affects how we interact with others. When we practice mindfulness, we nurture empathy and compassion, which enhances our relationships. By being present and attentive, we foster deeper connections and make decisions that consider the needs and feelings of those around us. This collaborative approach enriches our lives and creates a supportive environment where open dialogue and understanding can thrive.

In a world that often prioritizes speed and efficiency, the practice of mindfulness stands as a powerful act of self-care and awareness. By adopting a mindful approach to decision-making, we empower ourselves to be more intentional in our choices. We learn to listen not only to external influences but also to our inner wisdom, guiding us toward decisions that resonate with who we truly are.

As we navigate the complexities of life, let's remember that mindfulness is a valuable ally in our decision-making journey. By cultivating awareness, we create the space to reflect, evaluate, and choose with clarity and purpose. In this path of self-discovery, may we find the courage to make decisions that honor our authentic selves and lead us toward a more fulfilling and meaningful life.

In the grand scheme of life, each choice is a thread in our unique story. By practicing mindfulness, we can infuse each thread with purpose and intention, weaving a narrative that reflects our true essence. The journey of mindful decision-making isn't just about reaching a destination; it's about appreciating the richness of every moment along the way. Through this mindful perspective, we uncover not only the power of our choices but also the beauty of the journey itself.

Reflection Techniques: Journaling and Meditation

When it comes to understanding ourselves better, many of us might not realize just how powerful reflection can be. It's more than just looking back; it's a way to move forward with purpose and insight. Journaling and meditation are two wonderful methods that can help us reflect on our lives. Though they may seem different, they share a common goal: to help us dig deeper into our thoughts, desires, and ultimately, our choices.

Think of journaling as a blank canvas for your thoughts and feelings—a safe space where you can let it all out without fear of judgment. It's like sitting down with a good friend who listens without interrupting or critiquing. That's the beauty of journaling; it's a private chat with yourself. This practice encourages you to explore your mind and uncover the feelings and experiences that shape who you are.

You might start your journaling journey by reflecting on key moments that have influenced your life. What choices have led you to where you are now? By thinking back on these times, you can dig into what drove your decisions. Were they made out of fear? Inspired by ambition? Or perhaps a genuine desire to connect with others? Putting your thoughts on paper slows everything down, giving you the clarity you need to understand your motivations better.

Prompts can act like a guiding light as you write. For example, you could ask yourself, "What are my core values?" This simple question can open the floodgates to a wealth of insights. You might realize that values like integrity, creativity, compassion, or adventure aren't just fancy words—they're woven into your daily choices. As you reflect on this, you may start to notice patterns in how you make decisions, whether those choices align with your true values or not.

Another helpful prompt could be, "What themes keep cropping up in my past choices?" This exercise allows you to take a step back and look at your life as a whole. Are there choices you find yourself making repeatedly? Maybe you often prioritize what others think over your own feelings or avoid taking risks. As you write, pay attention to how the pen feels against the paper; let your thoughts flow freely while you gain a deeper understanding of yourself.

Free writing is another effective journaling technique. Here, you set a timer and write continuously for a set amount of time—be it five, ten, or even twenty minutes. The goal is to let your thoughts pour out without overthinking. You might uncover hidden desires or fears that have been lurking below the surface. With no structure or judgment to hold you back, you might just stumble upon important insights that lead to self-discovery. It's a freeing experience that lets you uncover truths that might be hard to express in the hustle and bustle of everyday life.

Now, let's shift from the written word to the peaceful practice of meditation. This method complements journaling beautifully. Meditation is all about finding stillness, helping you dive deeper into self-exploration. When you meditate, you quiet the noise in your head and tap into a deeper part of yourself. While journaling helps you put your thoughts into words, meditation encourages you to listen to your inner voice.

Meditation offers a wealth of benefits for reflection. When you sit quietly, focusing on your breath or a mantra, you create a peaceful space for your mind amid the chaos of life. It's like clearing out clutter in your living room to reveal a beautiful piece of art that was hidden beneath distractions. This newfound clarity enhances your ability to reflect on your experiences and decisions with fresh eyes.

To illustrate how meditation can transform your life, let's think about Sarah. A few years back, she felt completely lost, overwhelmed by work and personal relationships. Though she was successful on the outside, she felt unfulfilled. After discovering a meditation course, she decided to give it a shot. With consistent practice, she learned to simply sit with her thoughts, observing them without any judgment. Over time, Sarah realized that the frantic pace of her life had drowned out her true desires. By quieting her mind, she uncovered a passion for art that she had put on the back burner for too long. Armed with this clarity, she shifted her career direction and began chasing her artistic dreams, leading her to a richer and more fulfilling life.

Getting started with meditation doesn't have to feel overwhelming. Just keep it simple. Try to carve out just five minutes a day to sit in silence. Find a cozy spot, close your eyes, and focus on your breathing. Visualize inhaling positivity and exhaling negativity. If your mind starts to wander—and it probably will—just acknowledge the thought and gently bring your focus back to your breath. With practice, you'll find that these moments of stillness can become a nurturing space for clarity and insight.

As you blend journaling and meditation into your life, you create a very powerful approach to self-reflection. Each method complements the other, giving you a fuller understanding of your inner self. While journaling helps you articulate your thoughts and feelings, meditation provides the quiet space to process and absorb those insights.

Building a personal reflection routine that combines both techniques takes some intention and commitment. Start by creating an environment that nurtures introspection. Pick a quiet room filled with natural light, perhaps decorated with plants or calming artwork. Make it your special sanctuary where you feel safe to explore your thoughts.

Setting aside specific times for reflection is just as important. Just like you schedule meetings or events, make time for yourself. Whether it's early morning, during lunch, or right before bed, find a moment that feels right for you. Consistency is key; with time, this practice can become a cherished part of your daily routine.

As you delve into this journey of reflection, keep a curious and open mindset. Remember that your thoughts and feelings are valid, and exploring them can lead to greater self-understanding. Approach each journaling session and meditation with the aim of learning rather than judging. This gentle mindset opens the door to a deeper exploration of your inner world.

Creating your reflection practice not only empowers you to make choices that are rooted in self-awareness but also builds resilience. When faced with challenges, the insights gained from your reflective practices can serve as your guiding compass. Take Sarah, for example. Her meditation practice helped her pinpoint her passion and equipped her with the tools to tackle self-doubt and obstacles throughout her journey.

You can further enrich your reflection techniques by incorporating other practices into your routine. For instance, consider taking nature walks as a form of moving meditation. The rhythm of your steps can mirror the flow of your thoughts, allowing you to reflect while connecting with the natural world. Alternatively, explore creative outlets like painting or music to express your reflections in fresh ways.

As you grow your reflection practice, think about sharing your experiences with others. Join a discussion group, attend workshops, or even share your journaling insights with a trusted friend. Talking about your reflections can deepen your understanding and provide new perspectives—transforming solo practices into enriching community experiences.

The journey of self-reflection isn't a straight path; it's a winding road filled with discoveries, challenges, and moments of clarity. Embrace the beauty of this journey, and remember that every insight gained is a stepping stone toward a more intentional and authentic life.

In the grand picture of your life, journaling and meditation connect the threads of self-discovery and awareness. They equip you to navigate the complexities of decision-making with grace and help you make choices that truly resonate with who you are. As you practice these techniques, may you uncover the depths of your desires and motivations, ultimately guiding you toward a life that is not just lived but truly experienced with intention and fulfillment.

Chapter 10: Empowerment Through Informed Choices

The Path to Personal Empowerment: Making Informed Choices

Imagine standing at a crossroads with a large sign ahead, pointing in different directions. Each path promises a unique adventure, challenge, and reward. This scene represents not just a physical journey, but also the many decisions we face every day. Every choice we make, big or small, is shaped by our preferences, biases, and the influences around us. But realizing these forces exist is only the first step; the real strength comes from understanding how to navigate them wisely.

At the core of making informed choices is a deep sense of self-awareness. It's about recognizing our internal compass—our values, beliefs, and desires. Self-awareness isn't just a trendy term; it's a powerful tool that helps us peel away the layers of societal expectations, emotional urges, and mental shortcuts that often cloud our judgment. By developing this awareness, we start to see ourselves and the world more clearly.

Let's think about choosing a career path. It's easy to get overwhelmed by what others expect—family, society, or even our friends. In the quest for approval, many people find themselves in jobs that don't truly resonate with what they want. Self-reflection can act like a guiding light in this fog. Asking ourselves questions like "What excites me?" or "Which skills do I enjoy using?" helps illuminate our true preferences and leads us to choices that align with what we genuinely value.

Connected to self-awareness is the idea of cognitive biases. These mental shortcuts can be useful, but they can also twist our view of reality and lead us off course. For example, confirmation bias is our tendency to look for information that supports what we already believe, which can blind us to other viewpoints or warn us when a choice might not be right. By recognizing these biases, we can start to counteract them. This might mean seeking out different opinions, questioning our own assumptions, and staying open to new ideas.

We also need to be careful of the temptation of instant gratification—a psychological trick that often makes us choose immediate pleasures over long-term happiness. This can show up in many ways, like treating ourselves to a shopping spree or picking junk food over a healthier meal. Enjoying small pleasures isn't wrong, but finding a balance is key. Long-term goals can feel overwhelming, and the journey to reach them might seem tough. However, by breaking these goals into smaller, manageable steps and rewarding ourselves along the way, we can train ourselves to enjoy the process just as much as the end result.

Another factor to consider is the impact of social dynamics. The opinions of friends, family, and cultural messages can create a lot of pressure on our choices, often pushing us to conform instead of acting according to our own values. This pressure is especially strong in the age of social media, where curated lives and filtered images create a seemingly perfect world that can distort our views on success and happiness. It's important to remember that everyone's journey is unique. Instead of feeling like we need to measure up to others, we should focus on our own paths.

Creating a strategy for informed decision-making can be incredibly empowering. Start by setting up a simple framework for making decisions. This could be as easy as making a list of pros and cons or using a more complex decision matrix to weigh the importance of different factors. This structured approach not only clarifies the impact of each choice but also helps clear away the emotional clutter that often comes with big decisions.

In today's world, where knowledge is more accessible than ever, gathering and evaluating information is crucial. This could involve doing research, consulting trusted sources, or chatting with experienced professionals in a certain field. The more informed we are, the less likely we are to be swayed by superficial influences or emotional reactions that can cloud our judgment.

Don't forget about the power of visualization. Picture the outcomes of your decisions; it can provide clarity and insights that simple reasoning might miss. Imagine the potential results of a choice, feel the emotions tied to each option, and see how they connect to your values. This mental exercise can reveal insights that guide your decision-making, lighting the way forward.

In addition to self-awareness, recognizing cognitive biases, and having an informed strategy, embracing resilience is vital. The journey of making informed choices will come with its share of setbacks and challenges. However, rather than seeing these as failures, we can view them as opportunities for growth and learning. Each stumble teaches us something valuable, refining our understanding of ourselves and the decision-making process. Being able to bounce back from these experiences strengthens our sense of empowerment, reminding us that we control our choices and can adapt when necessary.

The journey toward personal empowerment is ongoing and requires effort. It's a lifelong commitment to understanding ourselves, our choices, and the world around us. The more we practice self-awareness, critical thinking, and resilience, the more skilled we become at navigating life's complexities.

As we move forward, let's remember to create a supportive environment. Surround yourself with people who inspire and encourage growth. Engage in communities or discussions that challenge your thinking and broaden your horizons. The company we keep can significantly influence our choices and mindset, serving as either a boost to our empowerment or a roadblock to our progress.

One strong way to reinforce informed choices is through accountability. Whether it's sharing your goals with a trusted friend or finding a mentor, having someone to support you can make a big difference. This accountability helps solidify your commitment and provides a sounding board for your thoughts and decisions, ensuring you stay true to your values and goals.

Ultimately, our choices shape our stories. They come together to create the narrative of who we are and who we want to be. As we embrace informed decision-making, let's remember that empowerment isn't just a destination; it's an ongoing journey. Each choice we make carves out our path, and with a greater awareness and thoughtful effort, we can steer our lives toward what truly matters to us.

Think about the power of autonomy—the ability to make decisions based on what you believe, rather than outside pressure. This autonomy not only builds self-confidence but also gives us a deeper sense of fulfillment. When we understand the reasons behind our choices, we're better positioned to create a life that is genuinely ours. Whether it's picking a career, fostering relationships, or chasing passions, making choices that reflect our true selves leads to a richer, more meaningful life.

In the end, the journey of empowerment through informed choices is one of self-discovery and growth. It invites us to reflect, learn, and adapt. As we equip ourselves with knowledge, recognize our biases, and commit to intentional living, we take back control of our lives. This empowerment isn't just about making choices; it's about making choices that truly matter—choices that represent our deepest values and dreams.

So, the next time you find yourself at a crossroads, remember the tools available to you. Embrace self-awareness, challenge your cognitive biases, seek out information, and build resilience. The power to change your life is within reach, and with each informed choice, you step closer to living a life that truly reflects who you are and what you value.

The Path to Personal Empowerment: Making Informed Choices

Cognitive biases are like hidden forces tugging at our thoughts, subtly steering our decisions in ways we often don't notice. These biases shape how we see things, affect how we feel, and ultimately influence the choices we make. Grasping these biases is crucial as we work toward personal empowerment. Without this awareness, we risk getting caught up in misleading thinking that can lead us off course.

Let's kick things off with one of the most common culprits: confirmation bias. Picture this: you're thinking about buying a new electric vehicle. You've heard rave reviews from friends who own one, and you're already leaning in that direction. As you start your research, you naturally look for articles and reviews that support your positive feelings while brushing aside any negative feedback. This bias can distort your view, making you overlook valid concerns or other options. The real danger here is that confirmation bias narrows our understanding, keeping us from making balanced choices.

Think about a time when you experienced this bias. Maybe you held strong political views and only read articles that echoed your beliefs. It felt good, right? But at what cost? By filtering out different perspectives, we let our biases control our beliefs instead of searching for the truth. To break free from confirmation bias, make a conscious effort to seek out diverse viewpoints. Engage with ideas that challenge your own, read articles from various sources, and question your assumptions. This practice can broaden your understanding and lead to better decision-making.

Next up is the bandwagon effect, which thrives on social influence and peer pressure. Imagine a group of friends excitedly raving about a new restaurant, and suddenly, you feel the urge to join in. The buzz is contagious, but soon enough, you've jumped on the bandwagon without considering whether it fits your tastes. This effect isn't just limited to food; think about viral trends on social media, investments, or even lifestyle choices. The pull of popularity can cloud our judgment, leading us to make decisions based on what others are doing instead of what we truly want.

To counter the bandwagon effect, it's vital to cultivate your own sense of autonomy when making choices. Ask yourself questions like, "What do I really want?" or "Does this match my values?" This kind of self-reflection helps ensure your choices are authentic rather than just following the crowd. Remember, just because everyone else is doing something doesn't mean it's right for you. Focus on distinguishing genuine enthusiasm from outside pressure.

Anchoring bias is yet another mental trap that can skew our decision-making. This happens when we give too much weight to the first piece of information we hear, which can heavily influence our choices. For example, if you're shopping for a car and the first one you see costs $50,000, that price becomes an anchor against which you compare everything else. When you come across a car priced at $40,000, you might view it as a steal, even if it's still beyond your budget. Anchoring can prevent us from fairly and accurately assessing our options.

To escape the grip of anchoring bias, approach information with a critical eye. Make it a habit to explore multiple sources and gather a variety of data before making a decision. This will help you form a more well-rounded perspective, free from the limitations of first impressions.

Don't overlook the availability heuristic, which occurs when we rely too much on immediate examples that come to mind when assessing a situation. If you've recently read about a series of airplane accidents, you may overestimate the risks of flying, even though it remains one of the safest ways to travel. The vividness of recent stories can distort our perception of reality and lead to unnecessary fears.

To counteract the availability heuristic, actively seek out balanced information. Read beyond the headlines and look at the bigger picture. Recognizing that our perceptions can be influenced by recent experiences helps us make clearer decisions.

As we navigate this maze of biases, growing our self-awareness becomes a powerful ally in our journey toward personal empowerment. Think of self-awareness as a flashlight shining light on our thoughts, motivations, and behaviors. With greater self-awareness, we can spot the biases affecting our decision-making and take mindful steps to lessen their impact.

One helpful way to boost self-awareness is through personality assessments. Tools like the Myers-Briggs Type Indicator or the Enneagram can offer valuable insights into our behavior, strengths, and areas where we can grow. By understanding our personality types, we can see how they shape our choices and relationships. For example, if you find out you're an introvert who needs time alone, this awareness can help you make decisions about social commitments that respect your need for downtime.

Values clarification exercises also play an important role in enhancing self-awareness. Taking the time to think about what truly matters to you can guide you in your decision-making journey. Ask yourself questions like, "What principles do I value the most?" or "What brings me joy?" This reflective practice can reveal your core values, allowing you to align your choices with what resonates most with you.

Another great way to increase self-awareness is by seeking feedback. Reach out to trusted friends or colleagues and ask them to share their thoughts on your strengths and areas for improvement. Constructive feedback can shine a light on blind spots you may have missed, helping you understand your behavior and how it affects others. Welcoming feedback, even when it challenges us, is a vital part of our growth.

Now, let's talk about why gathering relevant information before making decisions is so important. In an age overflowing with data, it's easy to feel overwhelmed. However, approaching decision-making step by step can empower us to make choices based on evidence rather than just emotions.

One simple yet effective approach is to create a classic pros and cons list. By writing down the benefits and drawbacks of each option, you create a visual tool that helps clarify your thoughts, making it easier to weigh the positives against the negatives. This method not only organizes your thinking but also encourages you to consider aspects you might have overlooked at first.

For more complex decisions, a decision matrix can be incredibly useful. This framework helps you identify and prioritize the factors that matter most in a situation. By assigning weights to each criterion, you can objectively assess your options and see which one best fits your needs. The structured approach of a decision matrix reduces the emotional noise that can accompany significant choices, leading to more rational outcomes.

Scenario planning is another powerful technique for informed decision-making. Imagine you're thinking about changing careers. Instead of only focusing on the job market, visualize different scenarios: what would happen if you made that change, what challenges might come up, and how would it impact your life? By exploring potential outcomes, you create a roadmap that prepares you for various possibilities, helping you choose a path that aligns with your ambitions.

Knowledge is a vital asset when making decisions. Informed choices come from our ability to gather and assess information effectively. Research the options in front of you, get advice from trusted sources, and learn from others' experiences. The more information you have, the better prepared you are to navigate the complexities of your choices.

Visualizing potential outcomes can also enhance your decision-making. Picture the different paths you could take and the feelings tied to each choice. Imagine yourself in the future, having made each decision—what emotions come up? Does one option fill you with excitement while another leaves you uneasy? This exercise allows you to explore the emotional aspects of your decisions, empowering you to choose a path that reflects your true self.

Resilience is also key to making informed choices. Life isn't a straight line; it's filled with twists, turns, and unexpected challenges. When setbacks arise, see them as chances to grow instead of roadblocks. Every experience, whether good or bad, teaches us valuable lessons that sharpen our decision-making skills.

Consider the story of Sarah, a woman who pursued her dream of starting a bakery. She put her heart and resources into her venture but faced numerous challenges, from supply chain issues to fluctuating customer demand. Initially, these setbacks felt overwhelming. However, by embracing resilience, Sarah adapted her business model and learned from her experiences, ultimately finding her niche. Her journey illustrates how resilience helps us navigate obstacles with grace and creativity.

As you move forward on your path to personal empowerment, remember to create an environment that encourages your growth. Surround yourself with people who inspire, challenge, and uplift you. Engage in conversations that broaden your perspective and encourage critical thinking. The company we keep can greatly affect our decision-making journey, either supporting our progress or holding us back.

Accountability is another powerful tool for making informed choices. Share your goals with a trusted friend or mentor who can provide support and perspective. When you vocalize your intentions, you strengthen your commitment and create a network of support that helps you stay true to your values.

The choices we make are not just transactions; they weave together the story of our lives. Each decision reflects our dreams, values, and identity. As we embrace informed decision-making, let's remember that empowerment is a continuous journey of self-discovery and growth. Our choices shape who we are, and each informed choice brings us closer to a life that aligns with our deepest values and aspirations.

So, the next time you find yourself at a crossroads, equipped with the knowledge of cognitive biases and tools for self-awareness, take a moment to pause and reflect. Tap into the power of informed decision-making, and trust in your ability to create a narrative that is uniquely yours. Each step, each choice, draws you closer to a life that truly resonates with your authentic self. With awareness as your guide and resilience in your toolkit, you can confidently navigate the complexities of choice and emerge empowered on the other side.

Taking Action: Crafting a Life Reflective of True Values

Life is a series of choices, each one like a brushstroke on the canvas of our existence. But how often do we stop and think about the colors we're using? Are they bright and lively, showcasing our true selves, or are they muted shades influenced by others? To create a life that truly reflects our values, we need to go beyond just thinking about it—we need to take real action. The first step in aligning our choices with our core values is to clearly define what those values are.

Defining our core values is like writing our own personal mission statement, a declaration of what truly matters to us. This is more than just a list; it's a meaningful exploration of who we are. Start by thinking back on moments in your life when you felt completely fulfilled, energized, or excited. What were you doing? Who were you with? Often, our most powerful experiences can help uncover the values that really resonate with us.

To help make this process easier, you might want to use a values worksheet. Here's a straightforward template to get you started:

1. **List Your Top Five Values**: Take a moment to write down what you believe are your core values. Common examples are honesty, family, creativity, security, adventure, and community.
2. **Describe Each Value**: For each value, write down what it means to you personally. Why is it important? How does it show up in your everyday life?

3. **Evaluate Your Current Choices**: Think about your daily decisions—your job, your relationships, how you spend your free time. Do these choices match your values? If there are differences, what do they tell you about your current path?
4. **Set Intention-Based Goals**: Think of specific goals that align with these values. For example, if family is a top value, a goal could be to have weekly family dinners or game nights.
5. **Create an Action Plan**: Identify concrete steps to achieve your goals. This will be your map to help you stay true to your values.

Writing these values down gives you a clear reference point. Life can get noisy and distracting, but with your values defined, you can consistently find your way back to what matters most.

Moving from understanding to action needs a solid action plan. But don't worry—it doesn't have to feel overwhelming. Breaking it down into small steps can actually make the process enjoyable and empowering. One great way to start is by using the SMART criteria:

1. **Specific**: Clearly define your goal. Instead of saying, "I want to be healthier," say, "I will attend a yoga class three times a week."

2. **Measurable**: Attach a way to measure your goal so you can track your progress. For example, "I will read one book a month on personal development."
3. **Achievable**: Make sure your goal is realistic given your current situation. If you're working full-time, aiming to read five books a month might lead to frustration.
4. **Relevant**: Your goals should matter to you and connect with your core values. If travel is important to you, a relevant goal might be, "I will save $200 each month for a family vacation."
5. **Time-bound**: Set a deadline for your goals. Having a timeline creates a sense of urgency and accountability, like saying, "I will finish my online course by the end of the year."

With this plan, your dreams become real objectives that you can work toward confidently.

But even the best plans can hit some bumps along the way. Life can be unpredictable, and challenges may pop up that can throw us off course. It's wise to think ahead about possible obstacles and how to tackle them. For instance, if managing your time well is a struggle, you might try techniques like the Pomodoro Technique to boost your productivity and stay focused on your goals.

Also, don't hesitate to seek out support and resources that align with your goals. Whether it's joining a community group, finding a buddy to keep you accountable, or taking online courses, surrounding yourself with people who share your values can provide encouragement and motivation.

Inspiring change isn't just an abstract idea; it comes alive through real-life stories. Take David, for example. He was a middle-aged man stuck in a job that left him feeling unfulfilled. He decided to follow his passion for environmental sustainability. Leaving his stable job was scary, but he took careful steps—enrolling in online courses, networking with professionals, and gradually transitioning into a role in environmental consultancy. Sure, there were challenges—financial worries, self-doubt, and fear of failing—but David stayed committed to his values and transformed his career, finding deep satisfaction and purpose in his work.

Then there's Mia, who dreamed of being an artist but felt trapped by what society expected of her. After years of pushing her passion aside for a more conventional job, she finally took a leap and went to art school. Facing doubt from family and friends, Mia leaned on her values of creativity and self-expression to fuel her drive. Today, she runs her own successful studio, showcasing her art to grateful audiences. Her story shows how daring to take action, even when times are tough, can lead to a meaningful and authentic life.

These stories not only inspire us but also highlight the importance of accountability. Sharing your goals with others can create a sense of commitment. When we express our intentions, we invite our friends and family to support us while also holding us accountable to our values.

It's also key to celebrate your wins along the way. Recognize your progress, no matter how small, and reward yourself for sticking to your values. This positive reinforcement boosts your motivation and reminds you why you started this journey.

As you navigate your life, remember that every choice you make is an opportunity to shape your story. Embrace your journey with curiosity and a willingness to learn from both your successes and setbacks. Your life is a work in progress, and every decision can bring you closer to the masterpiece that reflects your true self.

The impact of making informed choices is huge. When you actively connect your decisions to your core values, you start a transformative journey toward fulfillment and authenticity. Choosing becomes a conscious practice, where each decision brings you closer to the life you truly want.

As we wrap up this chapter, take a moment to envision the life you want to create. Picture it vividly, like you're watching a movie of your own making. What scenes are unfolding? Who's in your life? What emotions do you feel? By engaging with this vision regularly, you strengthen your commitment to this path, inviting clarity and motivation into your daily life.

While crafting a life that reflects your true values, keep in mind that adaptability is crucial. The path to authenticity isn't straight; it's full of twists and turns. Embrace these changes as opportunities for growth, and don't hesitate to adjust your goals as you evolve.

The journey of self-discovery and informed decision-making is one that lasts a lifetime. Equip yourself with self-awareness, resilience, and accountability. By intentionally creating a life that resonates with your true values, you can not only build a fulfilling life but also inspire others through your example.

In the grand scheme of life, let your choices be the threads that create a colorful, vibrant existence reflecting the depths of who you are. Embrace uncertainty, nurture your dreams, and take bold steps toward a life that is uniquely yours. You hold the power to shape your story and pave the way for a future that aligns perfectly with your aspirations. So, set out and create the life you were meant to live—one thoughtful choice at a time.

Faye Chandler

www.ingramcontent.com/pod-product-compliance
Lightning Source LLC
Chambersburg PA
CBHW071052240526
45471CB00015B/1644